MAR 1 9 2014

Baghdad

Baghdad: The City in Verse

TRANSLATED AND EDITED BY *Reuven Snir*

FOREWORD BY *Roger Allen*
AFTERWORD BY *Abdul Kader El Janabi*

HARVARD UNIVERSITY PRESS

Cambridge, Massachusetts
London, England
2013

Library of Congress Cataloging-in-Publication Data

Baghdad : the city in verse / translated and edited by Reuven Snir ;
foreword by Roger Allen ; afterword by Abdul Kader El Janabi.
pages   cm
Selected poems from the early classical period through the 20th century.
Includes bibliographical references and index.
ISBN 978-0-674-72521-8 (hardcover: alk. paper)
1. Arabic poetry — Iraq — Baghdad.   2. Baghdad (Iraq) — In literature.
I. Snir, R. (Reuven) translator editor of compilation.   II. Allen,
Roger, 1942–   III. Janabi, 'Abd al-Qadir, 1944–
PJ8047.B25B34 2013
892.7'100835856747 — dc23
2013015281

TO MY LATE PARENTS,

who were born in Baghdad and were forced to leave their beloved city, and, until their early deaths, never recovered from the painful separation

Contents

Foreword

by Roger Allen

Baghdad, fabled residence of Harun al-Rashid in *One Thousand and One Nights* and now the capital of Iraq, was a purpose-built city constructed by the newly victorious Abbasid family, who assumed the Islamic Caliphate after the defeat of their predecessors in that function, the Umayyads. The Caliph al-Mansur initiated plans for the building project in 758, and actual construction started in 762 at the site where the twin rivers of Mesopotamia, the Tigris and Euphrates, come closest together in their joint journey to the South-East and the gulf. The plan called for a city in the form of a circle, and the completed Abbasid capital was long known as "the round city." At its center stood the Caliph's palace. For many centuries the city was fabled for its cultural and intellectual life throughout the vast expanse of the Caliph's dominions and indeed far beyond that, but the passage of time, the ever-changing pattern of dynasties, and the emergence of new political and cultural centers — Cairo, Qayrawan, Fez, Cordoba, Marrakesh, Rayy, Samarqand, and so on — meant that Baghdad gradually but inexorably lost much of its former luster. The final blow came with the sack of the city in 1258 at the hands of Hulagu Khan, commander of the invading Mongol armies. A thirteenth-century poet, Taqi al-Din ibn Abi al-Yusr, depicts the consequences: "Oh seekers of news about Baghdad, the tears will tell you: / No benefit from remaining here, the beloved has departed. // Oh visitors to al-Zawra', please do not come here. / Baghdad is no longer a refuge; no one is here anymore. // The crown of the Caliphate, the great monuments, / all has been burned to ashes." Little of that previously fabled city remains today, but its glories survive in recorded state through the writings of historians and the creative imaginings of poets, whence the current collection.

In this anthology of Arabic poetry in translation, Reuven Snir, whose family belonged to the renowned Jewish community of Baghdad and emigrated to Israel in 1951, traces the variegated life of the city in a chronologically arranged selection of poems and poetic extracts. Through the eyes of generations, indeed centuries, of poetry and poets, we get an intimate portrait of a city and its people. Even in the centuries before the city is sacked by the Mongols, poets pass rueful comment as its people find themselves in the midst of a war caused by the disastrous decision of Harun al-Rashid — the actual Caliph as opposed to his "persona" in *One Thousand and One Nights* — to divide the Abbasid dominions between his two sons, al-Amin and al-Ma'mun. But wars and conflict aside, the poets also celebrate the life of the city, the beauty of its vistas and those of surrounding areas, and occasionally the oppressive heat of summertime. We read the impressions and imaginings of famous poets and other writers from the city's period of greatest and widest renown — a veritable who's who from the Arabic literary heritage: Abu Nuwas — yet another figure made yet more famous by his role in *One Thousand and One Nights;* Ibn al-Rumi; al-Buhturi; Ibn al-Mu'tazz (the poet-critic of renown and reluctant one-day Caliph before his assassination); the Sufi al-Hallaj before his death by crucifixion; al-Tanukhi, judge and anthologizer; al-Sharif al-Radi, renowned poet and, like his brother, al-Sharif al-Murtada, member of the Shi'i community of the city; Abu al-'Ala' al-Ma'arri, the blind poet and master of the ascetic poem (*zuhdiyya*) — his name "Ma'arri" pointing to Syrian origins in the town of Ma'arrat al-Nu'man to which he was to return; Usama ibn Munqidh, illustrious chronicler of the Crusades; and Ibn al-'Arabi, most famous and heterodox of Sufi masters. The images that these and other figures convey of the city, its people, its districts, and its climate vary widely: two contemporaries in the eleventh century, for example, paint very different pictures: 'Ali ibn Zurayq Abu al-Hasan al-Baghdadi, for example, tells us that: "Alas, for me Baghdad is the entire world, / her people — the only genuine ones." Whereas for Abu Muhammad 'Abd al-

Wahhab al-Maliki: "Baghdad is a fine home for the wealthy, / but an abode of misery and distress for the poor." Usama ibn Munqidh describes the city and its people as: "Beautiful venue, high-minded people, / they are charming and generous." While, for Ibn al-'Arabi, "The most beloved of the cities of God, after Medina, / Mecca, and Jerusalem, is Baghdad."

Whatever the image of the "pre-Mongol" city conveyed by this panoply of great poets and other authors, everything changes following the disaster of 1258, a litany repeated throughout the ensuing centuries and encapsulated in the verses of the nineteenth-century poet 'Abd al-Ghani al-Jamil: "My condolences for Baghdad, what a town! / Once glory nested here; now, it has flown away." Arrived at the twentieth century, we encounter a more chronologically detached vision of the city's history in the words of the neoclassical poets. The Iraqi poet Jamil Sidqi al-Zahawi can invoke the glories of the ancient past as he bemoans the tyranny of a present that forces him to leave, while the twin Egyptian neoclassicists of the same era Ahmad Shawqi and Hafiz Ibrahim glorify — albeit from a distance — the cultural heritage of Baghdad's now-lost days of cultural efflorescence. For al-Zahawi's fellow-Iraqi colleague Ma'ruf al-Rusafi, it is the sight of Baghdad inundated by flooding rivers that arouses his sorrowful nostalgia.

The decades of the twentieth century were to have a major impact on Baghdad: the consequences of the First World War saw the establishment of an Iraqi monarchy under a British protectorate, and the aftermath of the Second World War saw the foundation of the United Nations, one of the first actions of which was to authorize the establishment of a Jewish State in response to increasing Zionist demands. The Baghdad Jewish community had been and was both large and influential, especially in the administrative and cultural sectors, and many of its children who were known to me personally and who were subsequently to move to Israel have expressed pride in the Jewish community's notable participation in those and other aspects of communal life. In that particular social context and the subsequent history of relations between Arabs and Israelis, the words of the Iraqi Jewish poet Anwar Sha'ul, who did not join the first exodus from Iraq to Israel in 1951 but remained in the country until 1971, seem particularly telling: "My heart beats with love of the Arabs; / my mouth proudly speaks their tongue. // Do they and I not share a common source? / The distant past drew us together." His Jewish colleague Mir Basri, similarly forced into reluctant exile, longs to be buried "Near my ancestors who have slept for ages / in Baghdad's soil . . ."

In 1958 Baghdad witnessed what was probably the most violent revolution — in fact, the first of a whole series of political and social upheavals — among the many processes of change in the Arabic-speaking world that during the 1950s and into the 1960s aimed at getting rid of colonial occupiers and founding new, postindependence societies and political systems. Such profound disruptions to the life of the different communities in Iraq (and elsewhere) were inevitably reflected in Arabic poetry — traditionally the literary mode of resort in times of crisis and transformation — and in the role of poets and literature. In Iraq, as elsewhere, the new regime — or, in the case of Iraq, regimes — failed to foster the kind of open society that many had aspired to, and the country's poets were at the forefront of those who reflected the new miseries of a fear-based land. Thus, while the Syrian poet Nizar Qabbani may have tried to raise some echoes of the past in his poems about Baghdad (and I myself witnessed him at the Marbid Festival in Baghdad in 1988 delivering a poem in praise of Saddam Husayn), Iraqi poets themselves — among the most famous and important of all modern upholders of the great tradition of Arabic poetry — were consistent in their opposition, a posture that, more often than not, necessitated their personal exile for extended periods. Badr Shakir al-Sayyab looks back at his homeland from across the gulf, in Kuwait; 'Abd al-Wahhab al-Bayyati replicates the earlier tradition of Arabic poetry by spending much of his career in Spain. In the context of an orchestrated normality of terror, it is the Syro-Lebanese poet Adonis who poses the vital question: "Can it be that 'no-return' is a homeland?"

The past quarter-century (I am writing these words in the last days of 2012) has brought further and even enhanced misery to this already troubled country of Iraq and its capital city in the forms of war, communal strife, and varieties of foreign interference. Iraq had earlier been a region that the Ottomans, perhaps wisely in retrospect, divided into three separate provinces based on the cities of Mosul, Baghdad, and Basra, each with its majority population. Subsequently, first the British and, more recently, the Americans have attempted to bring together the disparate tribal and religious communities of the larger Mesopotamian region into a kind of democratically organized nation-state. The implementation of these external, imposed strategies has clearly been problematic (to put it mildly), and the eventual outcome remains unclear, not least because of the continuing confrontation between Sunni and Shi'i interests both inside and outside the country itself. Faced with these crushing realities — the tyrannical regime of Saddam Husayn, ousted by "shock and awe" (as the initial American bomb-assault was termed) and the continuing civil unrest that has ensued, the poet Adonis, who in 1969 had excoriated the Iraqi regime as "a cage of words," now directs his ire in "Salute to Baghdad" at the invaders who claim to be conducting "a preventive war," and "with the help of God" at that. Like Adonis, poets from other countries and regions of the Arabic-speaking world put into poetic images their feelings about Baghdad and Iraq and their sense of outrage at the sufferings of its people, but it is hardly surprising that the most telling images should belong to the Iraqi poets themselves. Whether they write from exile — Sa'di Yusuf, Fadil 'Azzawi, and, more recently, Sinan Antoon, now teaching at New York University; from within the Iraqi community in Israel — Ronny Someck; or from within Iraq itself, the poets continue to celebrate Baghdad, their city. In spite of all adversities, they invoke childhood memories, depict the city's daily routines, describe in loving detail the ever-present river Tigris and its twin banks and bridges at different times of the day and night, and portray the loves, intrigues, and sufferings of its people. When the outside world brings to Iraq and its capital city a conflict that is inexplicable, unasked for, and devastating to the various communities who are forced to desperately seek modes of survival, the poets are there to describe the horrors involved and the hatred and resentment that such conflict provokes. In Faruq Juwayda's agonized words: "Children in grieved Baghdad wonder / For what crime they are being killed; staggering on the splinters of hunger, / They share death's bread, then they bid farewell."

And in the war's aftermath they and everyone else still look to a future that hovers somewhere in the broad expanse that separates hope from despair. Here, then, is a history of one of the world's most fabled cities, told in the words of its poets through the centuries. As readers learn of that lengthy and often troubled history through the colorful and sometimes strange imagery of poetry, may they come to empathize with the ongoing struggles of its peoples.

Preface

> Like camels in the desert, dying of thirst,
> while carrying the water on their back
>
> *Abu al-'Ala' al-Ma'arri (973–1058)*

My parents were born in Baghdad and were forced to emigrate to Israel in 1951. Two years later, I was born — a "Sabra," a native-born Israeli-Jew. I remember that my father was a great lover of Baghdad and ardent admirer of Arabic poetry. He used to tell me about his happy days in Baghdad on the banks of the Tigris. For my edification, he would punctuate his stories with Arabic verses, even though I understood little and cared even less. The Israeli educational system was Zionist-centered and had little room for competing or alternative world views. As a result, Arab-Jewish children were educated in schools to be hesitant toward the culture of their own parents; in this case "their culture" was the culture of "the enemy." There is no need to elaborate on the tense atmosphere in our home. I eventually learned Arabic at high school, but the language was taught through the lens of perceived Israeli national security needs — in the spirit of the slogan "know the enemy." My *tawba* (repentance) was very slow and gradual and was prompted primarily by *nadam* (regret). After my father's death, I tried to recall something of the verses he used to recite to me. There was one particular verse he had recited over and over again. I remembered that it had something to do with camels and water and the feel of its music was still with me, the melodic resonance of *al-kamil* meter. At long last I "rediscovered" the verse; it was probably the above verse attributed to the blind ascetic poet Abu al-'Ala' al-Ma'arri (973–1058), the poet whose *Risalat al-Ghufran (The Epistle of*

Forgiveness), according to some scholars, influenced the *Divine Comedy* of Dante (1265–1321).

On March 12, 2010, at Burdick's in Harvard Square, I met Sharmila Sen, executive editor-at-large at Harvard University Press, to discuss my "publication plans." Ten days before, she had e-mailed me to say that she had read the description of my current project at the Radcliffe Institute of Advanced Studies at Harvard "with some interest." Actually she came up with what seemed to me then to be a wild idea, one that had never been in my plans and probably would never have occurred to me: that I compose a history of Baghdad through the eyes of Arabic poets from the time of the founding of the city. At the time, as a fellow at the Radcliffe Institute, I was deeply immersed in a research project on Arab-Jewish identities and could not imagine taking on such a formidable project.

In retrospect, however, I do not understand why such a project had been so far from my mind, not only then, but throughout my entire academic career. Since I started studying the Arabic language and its literature, I have been in love with Arabic poetry, and for tens of years I have been translating Arabic poems into Hebrew and English. Looking back even further, throughout my childhood and until the early death of my parents (my father died in 1979, my mother in 1988), Baghdad was always in the air. My parents used to speak the Baghdadi dialect of Judaeo-Arabic at home, even though my brothers, my sister, and I always responded in Hebrew! My father would recount to us his memories from the golden age of the Jews in the City of Peace during the first half of the twentieth century — "how pleasurable it was on the banks of the Tigris!" And there was, as well, a real, palpable taste of Baghdadi life at our home: the delicious Baghdadi dishes my mother would cook every day; the riveting songs of the great singers, the Iraqi-Jewish Salima Murad (1905–74) and her Iraqi-Muslim husband, Nazim al-Ghazali (1921–63), to which our parents would listen, enthralled, over Arab radio stations.

It was only after I embraced the project that Sharmila had suggested to me that I "read" al-Maʿarri's verse (above) in a new light and understood what my late father had for so many years tried, unsuccessfully, to convey to me regarding my dismissive attitude toward my own cultural heritage and toward the city of Baghdad. I was, in fact, like those camels in the desert, suffering from thirst but unable and, in my case, unwilling, to quench the deadly thirst with water so readily at hand.

Starting the research for the book, I was amazed to find hundreds of poems about Baghdad, in both classical and modern sources, as well as in sundry poetry collections. Some of these poems were written by Baghdadi poets, others by "transient," actual or virtual, denizens of Baghdad, all great lovers of this fabled city. The task of selecting the poems for the anthology was very difficult; so were the attempts to strike a balance between different periods, particularly between the first centuries after the founding of Baghdad and the twentieth century, when Baghdad, for different reasons, became once more a central topic for Arab and international audiences.

Unfortunately, most of the modern poems about Baghdad are steeped in sadness, sorrow, and despair, and only rarely can one find glimpses of hope and cheerfulness. But Baghdad has already proved her ability to rise from the ashes of defeat, darkness, and destruction and live to fight again. In 1961 Adonis addressed Baghdad and promised her a new future: "Time laid itself on your hands. / The fire in your eyes / Swept away and spread to the sky." Nizar Qabbani followed him a year later: "What could I write about you in the books of love? / For love of you, a thousand books are not enough!"

The present book would never have been written without Sharmila Sen's strong belief that such a project should be carried out. She has been the motivational force behind this project and personally involved in this poetic enterprise over the last three years. Not only did she provide the idea for the book, but as editor, she has had a significant, active role in the process of selecting and revising the poems. I cannot find words to thank her enough for having motivated me to take this wonderful journey in the realm of poetry written about Baghdad. I also thank Heather Hughes, editorial assistant in humanities at Harvard University Press, for her dedication to the project and for all her help.

My deep thanks go to Dr. Roger Allen, professor of Arabic Literature and Comparative Literature at the University of Pennsylvania, for writing the foreword and for reading the entire manuscript of the book, as well as for providing me with numerous suggestions to improve the translations. I could not have thought of a better scholar-translator than Professor Allen to review the translations.

A special word of appreciation is due to the independent scholar and author Aviva Butt for her great help throughout the process of preparing the manuscript for publication. She read the entire manuscript several times and provided me with numerous suggestions for both the translated poems and the introduction. Her contribution to the poetical translation of the poems and to the introduction was very significant. Her dedication to the project was tremendous and arose from her strong belief in the necessity of publishing such a book.

I thank my dear friend Dr. ʿAli Hussein, professor of classical Arabic literature from my own base, the Department of Arabic Language and Literature at the University of Haifa, for his suggestions for improving the translations and his valuable contribution to them.

I thank my dear friend the Baghdadi poet Abdul Kader El Janabi for writing this book's afterword. The text, in fact a sort of prose poem, also contributed to the writing of the introduction. Actually, the afterword is seemingly only the beginning of a text that could go on expanding.

I would like to thank my two dear friends from the Hebrew University of Jerusalem, Dr. Meir M. Bar-Asher, Max Schloessinger Professor of Islamic Studies, and Dr. Albert Arazi, professor emeritus of Arabic Language and Literature, for reading the manuscript and providing me with invaluable suggestions.

Thanks are due to Dr. Muhammad Siddiq, professor of Arabic, Hebrew, and Comparative Literature at the University of California, Berkeley, for his superb suggestions for improving the style of several sections in the book.

My thanks go to Prof. Dr. Stefan Wild, Professor für Semitische Philologie und Islamwissenschaft at Bonn University, for turning my attention to several important sources where I could find various texts on Baghdad.

In addition, my thanks for their help are due to Dr. Bassam Frangieh, professor of Arabic at Claremont McKenna College in California, and the writer and translator Stefan Weidner, editor-in-chief of *Fikrun wa Fann / (Art & Thought)*, published by the Goethe-Institut.

My gratitude also goes to the Baghdadi poet and scholar Dr. Sinan Antoon, professor at the Gallatin School of Individualized Study, New York University, for his valuable comments and for his suggestions for improving some poems.

My thanks are also offered to Dr. Joseph Zeidan, professor of Arabic Literature and the director of the Arabic Program at Ohio State University, for important references, particularly for female poets; to Dr. Raif Georges Khoury, professor of Islam Science at Heidelberg University, for his suggestions; and to Dr. Joseph Sadan, professor of Arabic Literature at Tel Aviv University, for his good advice.

I also thank the author and scholar Dr. Tabish Khair, professor at the Department of English, University of Aarhus in Denmark, and the poet Adam Sol, professor of English at Laurentian University, Georgian College, for their help at the start of the project. And I thank Dr. Susan Einbinder, professor of Hebrew and Judaic Studies and Comparative Literature at the University of Connecticut in Storrs, for her moral support and good advice throughout the project.

This has been one of the most enjoyable projects of my academic career. The whole process of researching, selecting, and translating was very pleasurable, and the results are the fruit of pure love. My hope is that the present anthology succeeds in capturing the spirit of Baghdad throughout her history. I have never been to Baghdad, but now, after three years of close companionship with her, albeit through the eyes of her amorous poets, and before moving on to another project, I empathize with al-ʿAbbas ibn al-Ahnaf when he wrote, "I left her though she was the eye's greatest delight; / I left my heart there hostage."

Translator's Note

All poems in this anthology until the beginning of the twentieth century (and sometimes even beyond) were originally written in the *qasida* form, which had been developed in pre-Islamic Arabia and perpetuated throughout Arabic literary history. The *qasida* is an elaborately structured ode of varied length that maintains a uniform meter and rhyme scheme throughout the entire poem. The opening line gives away the scheme in that both the first hemistich (half-line) and the second share the same end rhyme.

The *qasida* poems selected here are seldom translated in full because often only fragments are available. Generally, the autonomous nature of the meaning of each verse of the *qasida* allows the verse to stand alone. The translation aims to preserve this structural feature by translating each verse as a single autonomous unit consisting of a *(sadr)*, or first hemistich, that is paired with the *('ajuz)*, or second hemistich. For such poems I occasionally encountered several versions, and the order of the verses in each version was sometimes different. In such cases I often chose the version that most lent itself to translation. This "license" is obviously unavailable to modern poems in "free verse" or the prose poem. Therefore, when there are omissions in a modern poem, I insert the word *excerpts* after the title.

All but four poems are translated directly from the Arabic. The exceptions are: Ronny Someck's three poems originally written in Hebrew but subsequently translated into Arabic, thus becoming, in a sense, Arabic poems; the fourth poem, "Bildung," by Abdul al-Kader El Janabi, was originally written in English. Roger Allen's translation of "Death the Fox" is used by permission. Unfortunately, I could find only two relevant poems that might be attributed to female medieval poets and could be included in the present anthology. From the modern period, I included ten poems by eight female poets, all of them from the second half of the twentieth century.

The anthology is organized chronologically. Anonymous poems have been arranged according to content as well as sources. This arrangement may impart to the anthology a slightly random quality, especially when compared with anthologies that might be structured according to themes (nature, love, war, etc.), personalities (Harun al-Rashid, al-Amin, Hulagu, Saddam Husayn, etc.), or specific events (the civil wars, the Mongolian occupation, the Gulf Wars, the American invasion, etc.). The chronological order adopted here aims to access the "spirit of the city" and will, I hope, turn readers into "travelers-in-time," visiting and revisiting the Baghdads of the last twelve hundred fifty years.

With most of the poems from the classical period until the beginning of the twentieth century, it is difficult to pinpoint the exact date of composition. The dates of the poets' births and deaths thus frame the time scheme, unless a specific year, or event, is mentioned elsewhere. For poems from the twentieth century, in general, I note at the end of each poem the date of composition or publication.

Most of the modern poets whose poems appear in this anthology were born in Baghdad or spent significant periods of their lives there. Some of them are from other nation-states, generally writing their poems after visiting Baghdad. There are a few poems that are not directly about Baghdad but nonetheless warrant inclusion in the anthology either because their authors are Baghdadi, and identified with Baghdad, or because of the symbolical nature of their poetry. This is the case, for example, with poems by al-Husayn ibn Mansur al-Hallaj, a medieval poet, and Sinan Antoon, of the late twentieth century.

In the sources, classical poems never appear with titles. For the sake of convenience, I have added titles in square brackets. This might be considered to be an "intervention" in the poetic work since a title is a microtext, performing an important role along with the main text of the literary work in the reading process and the determination of its polyvalent meaning. There-fore, I have generally chosen "simple" titles, the simplicity or complexity thereof being a function of the title's relation to the text itself. If the relation of the title to the text is straightforward and readily accessible to the reader, it can be classified as "sim-ple." Conversely, if that relation is ambiguous, or obscure, and requires an effort on the part of the reader to disentangle its ambiguity, the title can be classified as "complex."

Names of poets are transcribed according to the usual professional transliteration but with no macrons. There are a few exceptions with poets who became well known to English readers by different names, such as Adonis instead of Adunis, Sargon Boulus instead of Sarkun Bulus, Abdul Kader El Janabi instead of 'Abd al-Qadir al-Janabi, 'Abd al-Rahman Touhmazi instead of 'Abd al-Rahman Tuhmazi, Murad Michael instead of Murad Mikha'il, and Sinan Antoon instead of Sinan Antun. However, in the references, I have used the precise translitera-tion but, again, with no macrons.

Because of the publisher's considerations, all references for the original Arabic poems have been removed. Readers who wish to locate the Arabic poems are encouraged to consult the References list. For the medieval period, if the *diwan* (complete works) of a poet is not mentioned in the list, the poem is proba-bly found in at least one of the following sources: al-Tha'alibi 1885; al-Khatib al-Baghdadi 1931; al-Subaki 1964–68; al-Washsha' 1965; al-Kutubi 1974; al-Suyuti 1976; Sa'di 1980; al-Alusi 1987; al-Dhahabi 1988–2004; Yaqut 1990; Ibn Taghribirdi 1992; Matlub 1994; al-Isfahani 1997; Marun 1997; 'Abd al-Rahim 2003; al-Jazrawi 2005; al-Jawari 2006; Ibn al-Fuwati 2003; Ibn al-Fuwati 2008; al-Mashhadani 2009; 'Awwad 2010. Modern poems can be found in the collections of the relevant poets mentioned in the References list. Many poems, or at least various verses from them, may be located by searching, in Arabic, for the name of the poet with the word *Baghdad* on the Internet.

Baghdad

Introduction

"Poetry and Baghdad are indivisible, flowing together. One re-flects, then feeds the other and so on," writes contemporary Baghdadi poet Abdul Kader El Janabi (b. 1944) in his after-word: "The very nature of Baghdad strikes the match that ignites the poetic imagination of the Iraqis, and in a sense, of poets in the Arab world." In the late 1920s, historian Reuben Levy wrote that even in the storied East there are few cities that hold the imagi-nation like Baghdad, "whose annals should be sought not in the humdrum narratives of the scribe but in the unfettered imagery of poet or painter."[1] Cities are "living processes" rather than "products" or "formalistic shells for living,"[2] but Baghdad has been shaped also by the numerous poets who have written about the city during the last 1,250 years. Surely, there are not many cities in the world about which so many verses have been writ-ten over such a span of time!

There were, of course, variations in the volume and nature of the productive creativity of Baghdad's poets. In the first few centuries after the city was founded, the world witnessed Bagh-dad's great cultural and artistic achievements and the inspira-tion of its very many poets and writers. In other periods, such as the 1920s–1930s, Baghdad became known for its remarkable reli-gious tolerance, multicultural cosmopolitan atmosphere, and peaceful cohabitations between all components of the society. There were also periods when Baghdad claimed attention because of its dramatic decline and disintegration, for example, after the thirteenth-century Mongol destruction; during Saddam Hus-ayn's ill-reputed regime; and, for being a theater for bloody wars, such as the Iran-Iraq war of the 1980s, followed in the next decades by the Gulf War and the American occupation. How-ever, even during periods when Baghdad seemed to be in the pro-cess of collapse and disintegration, the image of an alternative, utopian Baghdad, as metaphor, remained immune to vicissitudes of time and the dreary reality of the earthly city. The sway of Baghdad, the fabled city of Harun al-Rashid and the enchanted land of *A Thousand and One Nights,* will probably continue to capture the imagination of successive generations of poets, writers, and artists the world over. Neither East nor West seems immune to its irresistible charm.

Baghdad was founded at a time when Arabic poetry was at its peak. The development of the city thus coincided with, and was inspired by, the creative imagination of the poets who were associated with what was a great cultural urban center during the golden age of medieval Arabic culture. The glorious image of the city perched on both banks of the Tigris ignited the imagination of subsequent generations of poets to carve it in verse and enshrine it in the mantle of universal myth.

Soon after the founding of the city, it became obvious that a specific identity, with distinct characteristics of Baghdad and its residents, was coming into being. The Bedouin nomadic ideology, which retained influence even in the early urban centers of the Islamic empire, placed genealogy (*nasab*) far higher on its meritorious scale than homeland (*watan*) — the implication being that "place" was, at best, only secondary and perhaps even incidental to the constitution of identity. Thus, biographical dictionaries were organized according to profession, legal school, or generation, and only rarely according to city; it is no wonder that one of the outstanding examples of that type of dictionary was *Ta'rikh Baghdad (The History of Baghdad).* With the city of Baghdad, the relationship of a person to a place had acquired new meaning and became a formative constituent of individual identity — place and self became mutually interdependent, the one a reflection of the other. Abu 'Abd Allah al-Shafi'i (767–820), for example, illustrates the change in the attitude toward the place when he writes: "I have never stayed in a place which I did not consider a mere stage in a journey, until I came to Baghdad. As soon as I entered the city, I, at once, considered it was my very homeland."[3] Not only did the city of Baghdad begin to serve as a source of identity for Arab and Muslim alike, but the

Tigris and major icons of the city, such as various quarters, mosques, and palaces, became anchors of personal identity. Baghdad became not only one of the most impressive cities in the Islamic empire but also a place where people literally defined their identity in relation to it.[4]

As expressed in a truism from English poet William Cowper (1731–1800), "God made the country, and man made the town."[5] And like people, cities often have multiple layers of identity. Reflection on the subject of identity generally proceeds along one of two major premises: primordialist and nonprimordialist. The first assumes that there is an essential content to any identity that is defined by common origin or common structure of experience. The second argues that identities are constructed through an interplay of cultural reproduction, everyday reinforcements, as well as institutional indoctrination. In the present case, it seems that Baghdad's identity has been acquired through its natural location, rulers, residents, historians, writers, and, of course, its poets. However, since cities, especially major ones like Baghdad, are more evolving "processes" than finished "products," they inevitably embody, express, and prioritize specific values. And this is how a city comes to acquire its particular ethos or "soul." "Ethos" can be defined as the characteristic spirit of a culture, era, community, or place as manifested in its beliefs and aspirations; in other words, "ethos" is "the set of values and outlooks that are generally acknowledged by people living in any specific city." Cities not only reflect but also "shape their inhabitants' values and outlooks in various ways."[6] In the case of Baghdad, from its inception, the city was more than the sum total of its parts. From its golden age, its image has been shaped by the poetic creativity of its residents, visitors, and those who identified with it.

Daniel Bell and Avner de-Shalit studied the identity and "spirit" of contemporary cities. They concluded that Jerusalem, for example, is the city of religion; Montreal, the city of language; Oxford, the city of learning; Berlin, the city of (in)tolerance; Paris, the city of romance; and New York, the city of ambition.[7] What might we say about Baghdad's spirit? Or, should we refrain from any such attempt lest by reducing it to a single ethos, we end up being guilty of reductionism and simplification? And what might we add if we tried to judge Baghdad not only by viewing it from the perspective of "our global age," as Bell and de-Shalit have done with the aforementioned cities, but from the perspective of this city's history since its foundation in the eighth century? Does Baghdad actually have any particular ethos? If we should attempt to designate an ethos for the city, and ignore the controversy about the essence of "Islamic city," there is no doubt that, from the time of its founding, and in contradistinction to the aforementioned cities, Baghdad cannot be reduced to a single universal ethos that may serve as a recognizable core of identity shared by its inhabitants.[8] Nevertheless, Baghdad has been the city of Islam and Arabism *par excellence* — the center of the Islamic empire and the Arab world, in reality and certainly metaphorically. Baghdad was at times a metaphor even for the entire East. It was the city of the *Arabian Nights,* the city of the golden age of Islamic and Arab culture. Its destruction in 1258 reflected the decline of Arabism and Islam. For various Arab religious communities during the late nineteenth century and the first half of the twentieth century, it was the city of tolerance. By contrast, during most of the second half of the twentieth century, it was the city of Arab-Muslim dictatorship, or, during the last decades of that century, the city that illustrated the total submission of the Arab world and Islamic religion to the West.

Classical Arabic sources are full of references to the glory of the city as the capital of Islam and Arabism in the medieval ages. "Baghdad is the mother of this world and the queen of the provinces";[9] and "it is the navel of the globe, the treasure of earth, the source of sciences and the spring of wisdom."[10] When one person declared that he had never been to Baghdad, the answer was crystal clear: "In that case, you have seen nothing on the earth."[11] "Nothing is equal to Baghdad," said another, "for the sublimity of its rank, for the splendor of its authority, for the great number of its scholars and prominent personalities, and for its glorious poets."[12]

After he founded the city in 762, the Caliph al-Mansur (reigned 754–75)[13] called the new city *Madinat al-Salam* (City of Peace); this became the official name of the city on government documents and coins.[14] Later a shorter form of the name became popular, *Dar al-Salam* (Abode of Peace), a name that hints at the Qur'anic description of paradise: "And God summons to the Abode of Peace, and He guides whomsoever He will to a straight path; to the good-doers the reward most fair and surplus; neither dust nor abasement shall overspread their faces. Those are the inhabitants of Paradise, therein dwelling forever."[15] By the eleventh century, "Baghdad" had become the almost exclusive name for this world-renowned metropolis.[16] Most Arabic scholars have assumed the name "Baghdad" to be derived from Middle Persian, a compound of *Bag* (God) and "*dad*" (given), meaning "God-given" or "God's gift." However, the name *Bagdadu* was in use from the time of Hammurabi (1800 B.C.), which means that the name was current before any possible Persian influence. The city was also known as *Madinat al-Mansur* (City of al-Mansur); *al-Zawra'* (the bent, or the crooked);[17] and *al-Madina al-Mudawwara* (Round City), since the old city was built as a circle with an approximate diameter of between two and three kilometers. The city was planned so that within it there would be many parks, gardens, villas, and promenades, and at its center would lie the mosque and headquarters for guards. The four surrounding walls of Baghdad were named Kufa, Basra, Khurasan, and Damascus after the destinations to which the city gates pointed.

After its founding, the city was developed rapidly. "Never had there been a Middle Eastern city so large," Ira M. Lapidus writes. "Baghdad was not a single city, but a metropolitan center, made up of a conglomeration of districts on both sides of the Tigris River. In the ninth century it measured about twenty-five square miles and had a population of between 300,000 and 500,000. It was ten times the size of Sasanian

Ctesiphon." Baghdad was larger than Constantinople or any other Middle Eastern city. In its time, Baghdad was the largest city in the world outside China.[18] With the founding of Baghdad, the Islamic empire established an effective governing system such as had never before existed: it had political, military, juridical, and administrative powers, talented bureaucratic staffs, and improved practices. For example, the office of the vizier was further developed at the time, and his power, as chief of administration, functioned in direct connection to the wishes, or one could say the strength, of the caliph. For example, the Barmakid viziers were very powerful at the time, but Harun al-Rashid did not hesitate to execute prominent members of this family.

Many passages in classical literary sources, prose and poetry, testify to the unique nature of Baghdad. A short while after its founding, Abu 'Uthman 'Amr ibn Bahr al-Jahiz (776–869), one of the greatest of classical Arab authors, gave the following testimony: "I have seen the greatest of cities that are known for their perfection and refinement, in the lands of Syria and the Greeks and other countries, but I have never seen a city like Baghdad whose roofs are so high, a city which is so round or more noble, the gates of which are wider and the walls better. It is as if the city were cast into a mould and poured out."[19] When referring to the three great cities in the territories known today as Iraq, al-Jahiz made the observation that "industry is in Basra, eloquence in Kufa, but goodness in Baghdad."[20] Abu al-Qasim ibn al-Hasan al-Daylami related: "I have travelled throughout the lands, visited countries from the borders of Samarkand to Qayrawan, from Sri Lanka to the lands of the Greeks, but I have never found a place better than or superior to Baghdad."[21]

Baghdad acquired acceptance as the urban center of the Arab world and Islamic empire, to the degree that people regarded all other places outside it as rural:[22] "Baghdad is the metropolis of the world," Abu Ishaq al-Zajjaj (d. 923) said. "Outside it, there is only desert."[23] When a visitor returned from Baghdad, he was asked about the city and replied, "Baghdad among the lands is like a master among slaves."[24] The traveler al-Maqdisi al-Bashshari (947–90) described Baghdad as having "a nature and elegance peculiar to her, excellent faculties and tenderness; the air is soft; the science is precise; everything is good. Everything nice is there; every wise man comes from there. Every heart longs for this city. Every war is declared against her. Her fame defies description, her goodness cannot be depicted. Praise cannot reach her heights."[25]

As the capital of the Islamic empire, it is no wonder that Baghdad has been praised as a religious center: "Baghdad is the City of Peace; alas she is the city of Islam," Abu al-Faraj al-Babbagha (925–1008) wrote. "The Caliphate of Islam nested there, hatched and struck its roots into the earth, and made its branches tall. Her air is more pleasant than any other air and her water sweeter than any other water, and her breeze is softer than any other breeze."[26] It was said that whenever the name of Baghdad was raised in any conversation, people quoted the Qur'anic verse: "A good land, and a Lord All-forgiving."[27] An interpreter explained that Baghdad was enriched with the fruits of a refreshing breeze.[28] "Baghdad is a paradise on earth," we read in the sources, "the City of Peace; the dome of Islam; the union of two rivers; the head of the land; the eye of Iraq; the house of the caliphate; the ingathering of good deeds and actions; the source of uncommon qualities and niceties. There can be found experts in any of the arts and extraordinary people in every field."[29] Also: "From the merits of Islam — Friday in Baghdad, the prayer performed during the nights of Ramadan in Mecca, and religious festivals in Tarsus."[30]

Moreover, Baghdad enjoyed a pluralistic, cosmopolitan, and multiconfessional atmosphere with multicultural, ethnic, and religious gatherings of Muslims, Christians, Jews, Zoroastrians, pagans, Arabs, Persians, various Asian populations, and so on. This atmosphere was initially inspired by the leadership of the Caliph al-Mansur (reigned 754–75), who propagated, from Baghdad, an open and multicultural policy toward religious minorities. The political, religious, and cultural supremacy of Baghdad as the center of the flowering Islamic empire encouraged such an atmosphere throughout other close and even remote cities. A contemporary text describing a gathering in the southern city of Basra in the year 156H (A.D. 772–73), may serve to illustrate this policy of multiculturalism:

> Ten persons used to meet regularly. There was no equivalent to this gathering for the diversity of the religions and sects of its members: al-Khalil ibn Ahmad — a Sunni, and al-Sayyid ibn Muhammad al-Himyari — Shiite, and Salih ibn 'Abd al-Qaddus — dualist, and Sufyan ibn Mujashi' — Khariji, and Bashshar ibn Burd — morally depraved and impudent, and Hammad 'Ajrad — heretic, and the exilarch's son — a Jew, and Ibn Nazir — a Christian theologian, and 'Amr the nephew of al-Mu'ayyad — Zoroastrian, and Rawh ibn Sinan al-Harrana — Gnostic. At these gatherings they used to recite poems, and Bashshar used to say: Your verses, Oh man, are better than *sura* this or that [of the Qur'an], and from that kind of joking and similar things they declared Bashhar to be a disbeliever.[31]

However, the glorious and multicultural cosmopolitan image of Baghdad, in the imagination of Arab culture, concealed a day-to-day reality of a city that suffered from all kinds of difficulties and troubles, just like any other medieval city. An example is that of the Caliph Harun al-Rashid (763–809), whose name and fame have been associated with Baghdad as the legendary ultimate capital of the Islamic empire. It was under him that Baghdad flourished and became the most splendid city of its period. Taxes paid by rulers were used to finance activities in fine art, the construction of buildings with a high standard of architecture, and also a luxurious and even corruptive way of life at court. Due to the One Thousand and One Nights tales, and particularly his activities in Baghdad, Harun al-Rashid became legendary. However, his true historic personality was thus obscured.

In 796, al-Rashid actually moved his court and the governmental offices from Baghdad to al-Raqqa in the mid-Euphrates region and spent most of his reign there. Occasionally he would spend time in Baghdad, and in one such instance he returned to al-Raqqa leaving behind one of his slave girls, whom he very much missed. He wrote some verses for her, among them: "Oh he who ill-treats himself, / leaving behind his beloved. // I will forgive my beloved, forgiveness is my nature, / I will not forgive myself." Then he gathered many singers with the request to set his verses to music. Twenty melodies were composed from which the caliph liked that of al-Zubayr ibn Dahman.

Harun al-Rashid was virtually responsible for dismembering the empire when he apportioned Baghdad between his two sons al-Amin (reigned 809–13) and al-Ma'mun (reigned 813–33). After his death, a civil war (*fitna*) broke out between them (811–13). Contemporary poets described the events of the civil war, and between their poetic lines, the high status of Baghdad is apparent. 'Amr ibn 'Abd al-Malik al-Warraq (d. 815) wrote, "Oh Baghdad, who afflicted you with an evil eye? / Were not you the eye's delight?" Another anonymous poet said: "I weep blood over Baghdad, / I lost the comfort of an elegant life. // Anxiety has replaced happiness; / instead of prosperity, there is only misery." And Ishaq al-Khuraymi (d. 829) described a *mundus inversus* situation: "The slave has shattered the pride of his master / and enslaved noblewomen. // Among the protégés, the noble have become the most evil. / He who had been afraid of roads has become the master." This is a description of a world upside down, reminiscent of the *Carmina Burana*: the Fathers Gregory, Jerome, Augustine, and Benedict are to be found in the alehouse, in court, or in the meat market; Mary no longer delights in the contemplative life, and Lucretia has turned whore.[32] No restraints were enforced in that cruel war between al-Rashid's sons. A graphic account is given in the verses of al-Husayn ibn al-Dahhak (778–870) when, addressing al-Amin, he says:

Among the violations of your sanctity they abused,
behind curtains, the Prophet's female descendants' honor.

Your relatives remained in their places and failed to help.
All of them admitted humiliation.

Their virgin females showed their ankles
in grief, as they wept their demand for justice.

Garments were stolen, veiled women
were exposed, earrings were removed.

While being assaulted they seemed as
pearls emerging from oysters.

Notwithstanding all, within a short time after its inception, Baghdad evolved into a significant industrial and commercial center for international trade as well as the intellectual and cultural heart of the Arab and Islamic world. On the latter level, Baghdad garnered a worldwide reputation as the "center of learning." In the Middle Ages, Baghdad housed several key academic institutions, the best known being Bayt al-Hikma (House of Wisdom). This high point of Islamic civilization came when scholars of various religions from around the world flocked to that city, which was the unrivaled center for the study of the humanities and sciences, including mathematics, astronomy, medicine, chemistry, zoology, and geography, in addition to alchemy and astrology. Drawing on Persian, Indian, and Greek texts, Baghdad's scholars accumulated the greatest collection of learned texts in the world and built on this knowledge through their own discoveries. In these times, there was also a market for copyists *(suq al-warraqin)* where more than one hundred booksellers' shops were to be found, and writers and merchants bought and sold manuscripts. Baghdad's libraries were renowned for their wealth even beyond the Arab world. Whereas the largest library in twelfth-century Europe housed around 2,000 volumes, there was a library in Baghdad that had 10,400 books.[33] In Umberto Eco's *Il Nome Della Rosa* (1980), the library of the abbey is praised as "the only light Christianity can oppose to the thirty-six libraries of Baghdad, to the ten thousand codices of the Vizier Ibn al-'Alqami."[34] However, Baghdad's rapid development met with delays. In 836 the caliphate residence was removed to the new city of Samarra, just built by the Caliph al-Mu'tasim (reigned 833–42). The caliphate would remain there for over fifty-five years, that is, until the year 892 when it was returned to Baghdad by the Caliph al-Mu'tamid (reigned 870–92). During that period, Baghdad missed the attention of the caliphs, even though it was still the center of commercial and cultural activity.

From the late tenth century, intersectarian conflicts between the Muslim Shiites and Sunnis became usual, but soon the population of Baghdad became international, a mixture of different religions, nations, and cultures. The Jews of Mesopotamia, for example, who for centuries spoke Aramaic, in which language they produced the Talmud, underwent a rapid process of Arabization and integration into the surrounding Arab-Muslim society, the majority of them congregating in the new metropolis of Baghdad. Facilitating their integration was their high level of achievement and resulting prosperity in commerce, education, and culture.[35] It is estimated that in the tenth century the population of Baghdad reached one and a half million and was considered to be one of the largest cities in the world, the kind of city that had not been previously known in the Middle East.[36] Very sophisticated services were installed to meet the requirements of its residents. This is illustrated by, for example, the health system. We know of hospitals existing in Baghdad as early as the ninth century. At the beginning of the tenth century, the chief court physician, Sinan ibn Thabit, was appointed director of the city's hospitals; he founded three additional ones.[37]

Many poems in the anthology reflect various levels of life in Baghdad throughout the first centuries after its founding and in a sense may be read as an alternative history of the city. "Literature is a frail vehicle for documentation," James Dougherty writes, "but it can become powerful when understood as the imaginative review of experience, a review that both discovers and imparts those spiritual expectations against which the city's appearance must be measured."[38] Moreover, the history of Baghdad, during its formative classical period, cannot be fully documented without poetry. This is all the more obvious since until the second half of the twentieth century, poetry was the principal channel of literary creativity and served as the chronicle and public register of the Arabs *(al-shi'r diwan al-'Arab)*.[39] No other genres could challenge the supremacy of poetry in the field of belles lettres across more than fifteen hundred years of Arabic literary history. This high status that poetry enjoyed in Arab society as a whole is reflected in a passage by the eleventh-century scholar Ibn Rashiq al-Qayrawani:

> When a poet appeared in a family of the Arabs, the adjacent tribes would gather together and wish that family the joy of their good luck. Feasts would be got ready, the women of the tribe would join together in bands, playing upon lutes, as they were wont to do at bridals, and the men and boys would congratulate one another; for a poet was a defence of the honour of them all, a weapon to ward off insult from their good name, and a means of perpetuating their glorious deeds and of establishing their fame forever. And they used not to wish one another joy but for three things: the birth of a boy, the coming to light of a poet, and the foaling of a noble mare.[40]

Poets of the time actually referred to Baghdad as a paradise on earth; they described its beauty, natural scenes, and the attachment they felt toward it. When the poet al-'Abbas ibn al-Ahnaf (750–809), for example, had to leave Baghdad, he wrote: "I left her though she was the eye's greatest delight; / I left my heart there hostage." Zubayda bint Ja'far, Harun al-Rashid's wife, asked Mansur al-Namari (d. 809) to compose verses that would evoke her love for Baghdad and he recited the following verses: "Tree branches in Baghdad, what a wonderful smell, / scores of lovely spots, to delight world and religion // Breeze reviving the sick, / blowing between sweet basil branches." Hearing him, Zubayda granted him at once two thousand dinars. 'Ali ibn Jabala al-Ansari (known as al-'Akawwak) (776–828) wrote that "Separating from her, I was Adam / expelled from Eden." 'Ali ibn al-Husayn al-Wasiti (d. 919) asked a rhetorical question and was quick to respond: "Is there any equivalent to the City of Peace?! / A miracle! You will not find for Baghdad any parallel. // A temple for the hearts, spring / there everlasting, even in summer." And 'Umara ibn 'Aqil (798–853) asked a similar question: "Have you seen in any corner of the world / a tranquil abode like Baghdad?!" In another poem he added: "There is nothing like Baghdad, worldly-wise and religious, / despite time's transitions." Ibn al-Rumi (836–96) depicted it as "A city where I accompanied childhood and youthfulness; / there I wore a new cloak of glory. // When she appears in the imagination, I see on her / budding branches aflutter."

The likes of Baghdad's residents are unavailable in other places, as 'Ali ibn Zurayq Abu al-Hasan al-Baghdadi (d. 1029) argued: "I have traveled far to find a parallel for Baghdad / and her people — my task was second to despair. // Alas, for me Baghdad is the entire world, / her people — the only genuine ones." And al-Tahir ibn al-Muzaffar ibn Tahir al-Khazin (tenth century?) declared: "Tender weather, balanced and healthy, / the water — what a taste! Sweeter than wine! // Her Tigris, two banks arrayed for us like pearls in a necklace, / a crown beside a crown, a palace beside a palace. // Her soil, musk; her water, silver; / her gravel, diamonds and jewels."

On the other hand, Baghdad was also known as a hedonist city, where pleasures of all sorts were available, particularly in its many palaces. Among these palaces, mention might be made of Qasr al-Khuld (Palace of Paradise), built in 773 by al-Mansur on a hill along the western bank of the Tigris. Surrounding Qasr al-Khuld were houses for the ruling family, as well as houses for the administrative officials and military officers and their families. These houses eventually became the neighborhood called al-Khuld after the palace. Al-Khuld neighborhood was known for the luxurious gardens and parks encircling it. Qasr al-Qawarir (The Glass-Vessels Palace) owned by Zubayda was also very special. One of the clerks of the time described this palace saying: "It was surrounded by a large garden with most types of birds and wild rare animals. The entrance hall was about 40 meters long and was covered with a jewel-studded carpet. The ceiling stood on pillars made of ebony decorated in gold. The walls were decorated with inscriptions of verses from the Qur'an, and all nails on the walls were made of gold." The palace of Ja'far al-Barmaki in al-Shamassiya was known for the creative way in which it was built. The palace, Qasr al-Taj (The Crown Palace), was another well-known place of interest. The Caliph al-Mu'tadid (reigned 857–902) had started its construction, but it was only his son al-Muktafi (reigned 902–8), who finished the work. During the reign of al-Muqtafi a fire broke out in it.

Descriptions of Baghdad's palaces were often complemented by descriptions of beautiful young women.[41] The pleasures, as 'Ali ibn al-Jahm (804–63) wrote, were sensual: wine parties, cupbearers, young men and women, and a *carpe diem* atmosphere, as at al-Karkh's Gate:[42]

> [U]se your hands, carefree.
> Do not be afraid of the master; do whatever you want.
>
> Hint with your hand, wink, do not fear
> any watcher if you are not niggardly.
>
> Keep a distance from the lamp — curse it;
> as soon as the lamp is extinguished, approach and kiss.
>
> Ask! — nothing is forbidden — say whatever you want;
> sleep with no fear; get up without any hurry.
>
> Exploit the days of your youth; all of them will pass
> and perish, disappointment will soon be revealed.
>
> Life is only a night whose end projects
> us into a day of hastened pleasure.

'Ali ibn al-Jahm wrote one of the most famous poems about Baghdad, known as the *Rusafiyya*, which is a praise ode presented to the Caliph al-Mutawakkil (reigned 847–61).[43] During the next centuries and up to our time, many poets would allude to its first verse in various intertextual manners as we can see in the present anthology as well:

Does' eyes between al-Rusafa[44] and the bridge
carried desire from places I know or know not.[45]

Homosexual love was very widespread and accepted in Baghdad at the time, and among the upper classes in society there was always an urgent need for newly imported young beardless boys. When Abu al-Ma'ali (1028–85) was suddenly seen with a bearded boy, eyebrows were lifted: "Look for another! they urged. / In that case I will never be pleased, I replied. // If his saliva were not honey, / the bees would never have invaded his mouth."

There were also poems written about the *'ayyarun* (lit. scoundrels), a term applied to certain warriors who were grouped together in Baghdad from the ninth to the twelfth centuries. They indulged in a rule of terror directed against wealthy people, pillaging shops and robbing houses. About one specific *'ayyar*, who belonged to a certain sub-group of the *'ayyarun*, that were *mukhannathun* (*mukhannath* — effeminate, homosexual, or hermaphrodite), Abu al-Fadl ibn Muhammad al-Khazin al-Katib (d. 1131) wrote the following verses: "I am scared of him when he is drunk; noticing my horror / he shows a dignified and sober face. // He is 'Antar; if you wish, he could be 'Ablah as well / a lion in war or a gazelle for copulation." 'Antar was a hero of well-known romances of chivalry and 'Abla was his sweetheart. The essential feature of the romances is to recall the figure of the poet 'Antara ibn Shaddad, sixth-century author of one of the Mu'allaqat (the oldest collection of complete ancient Arabic odes).

The hedonism of Baghdad's wealthier residents created a need for more free time for leisure. From the start, with the Abbasid dynasty, the caliphate's public offices were closed on

Fridays so that believers could pray together in the mosques. For rest, relaxation, and leisure, the Caliph al-Mu'tadid (reigned 857–902) added another off-day — Tuesday. Every Tuesday, public employees would stay at home or head for public parks where they would spend their time in recreation and rest. Sometimes, it seemed a shame for a man to stay in the house on Tuesday and not participate in the *majalis* (sessions) of singing and wine drinking. Various poets wrote about that weekly day of vacation, such as Ibn al-Rumi: "Tuesday? What is Tuesday? / It is raised high in the pick of the days. // A center in the middle of the week, / a pearl necklace decorating a beautiful woman."

This hedonist aspect of city living aroused opposition from ascetic and mystical circles that considered Baghdad a dangerous place because of its luxurious life and the shamelessness and excessive pleasures that newcomers could be tempted by — all of which could cause avoidance of religious observance and duties. For example, 'Abd Allah ibn al-Mubarak (736–97) held that if you want to be pious you should avoid Baghdad: "Please tell those preferring abstinence, / tell all considered to be pious: // Stay on the frontier, be modest; / Baghdad is not an abode for hermits. // Baghdad is a place only for kings, / an abode solely for hunters and knights." On the other hand, the ascetic poet and philosopher Abu al-'Ala' al-Ma'arri (973–1058), who was born in Ma'arrat al-Nu'man, had longed since childhood to live in Baghdad. He was, however, able to visit the city only when he was in the fourth decade of his life, at which time he immediately gained the appreciation of the cultural circles of Baghdad. Living in the city, however, he suffered from his misfortune [his blindness] and from the jealousy of his contemporary rivals. Some poems in the anthology relate to those experiences, such as the verses he wrote upon his parting from Baghdad addressing the Treasurer of the House of Knowledge in the city:

> Oh treasurer of the House of Knowledge, so many
> deserts

separate us, full of voices of demons and partridges.

If horses of speech bolt, you
can control them with their reins.

Fright never caused me to neglect your friendship;
there we should observe only discipline.

Maybe time will be satisfied and free me from my
   chains,
or perhaps it is always angry.

Like any other urban center, the city suffered from negative phe-
nomena such as social differences between the classes. Unlike
poets who described Baghdad as a city of only dreams, there were
other views such as this from the following anonymous poet:
"May God make rain fall upon Baghdad — what a paradise! / A
pleasure for souls! // Alas, only for the wealthy is it a dream. / For
the penniless, it is a heart-rending loss." And Abu Muhammad
ʿAbd al-Wahhab al-Maliki (d. 1031) had no doubts but that
"Baghdad is a fine home for the wealthy, / but an abode of misery
and distress for the poor. // I walked among them in dismay / as
though I were a Qurʾan in an unbeliever's house." Muhammad
ibn Ahmad ibn Shumayʿa al-Baghdadi (thirteenth century) cap-
tured the self-centered nature of this urban center's residents:
"Friendship of al-Zawraʾs residents is falsehood, / residents'
warmth as well — don't be tempted. // Baghdad is a place for a
mere 'How are you?' / You will not be able to gain more." And
Abu al-ʿAliya (ninth century) has strong advice: "Leave! Bagh-
dad is not a place to stay in. / There is no benefit from her. // She
is a place for kings, their wickedness seen in their faces, / all of
them devoid of any glory."

Many anonymous verses described the immoral and evil
nature of the residents: "I abhor Baghdad; I abhor life
there. / This is from experience, after a taste," says one anony-
mous poet. "Baghdad's residents have no pity for the needy, / no
remedy for the gloomy. // . . . People whose encounters are em-
broidered / with ornamented rhetoric and lies. // Abandoning

the path of nobility, / they rival each other instead in disobedience and sinfulness." And another adds: "It is a land where men's souls are sick, / the stench even more when it rains." And a third poet says: "May God rain on Baghdad; may He protect her; / alas, may the clouds not provide rain for her residents. // Mean as they are, amazingly so, / for goodness sake, why have they been allowed such a paradise?" And a fourth anonymous poet: "Enough of moaning, thank God. / I could not manage in Baghdad anymore. // I consort with people who afford me no pleasure. / I keep company with people I deem undesirable."

There were also corruptive phenomena, like those of the viziers. Take, for example, the vizier Abu ʿAli Muhammad ibn Yahya. He was known as a great opportunist and hypocrite. When he saw people praying, he would hurry to join them; when someone asked him for help, he would beat his breast and say, "With the greatest of pleasure." However, he gave nothing. That is why the people used to call him the Breast Beater. He was known for his hankering for bribes. When appointing officials, he did so only in exchange for bribes. At times he would appoint someone, and then, after a few days, regret it and accept a higher bribe from someone else. It is said that in al-Kufa in the course of twenty days he appointed and fired no fewer than seven governors. Describing this vizier, an anonymous poet wrote: "This minister — a minister in stupidity, / no sooner appointing than dismissing. // In his office, he assembles bribers and campaigners; / the best merchandiser is the winner. // I beseech you not to reproach him; / he barely escaped beggary."

It was in the prisons of Baghdad that (so we learn from poetry) the craft of weaving waistbands became very developed, and served as a metaphor for the deterioration of the status of the prisoners. We learn this, for example, from the poetry of a prince who succeeded in ruling for a single lone day before being strangled in a palace intrigue; ʿAbd Allah ibn al-Muʿtazz (861–909) writes: "In Baghdad, I got lessons in weaving waistbands. / Before imprisonment, I had been a king. // After riding noble horses, I was chained. / This is because of changing constellations." In a letter to a friend, he complains that

> The sky in your town [Baghdad] is dirty, her water and air are muggy, her weather dusty, her soil quagmire, her water clay, her dirt of dung, her walls unstable, her October is like July — many are burnt by the sun. In the shed the sweat is unbearable, her houses narrow, her neighbors evil, her citizens wolves, their speeches curses, their beggars deprived, their money hidden, never for spending, never for releasing, their gardens know no gardening, their roads rubbish, their walls shabby, their houses cages.

And he composed the following verses: "In Baghdad, night made my sorrow deepen. / If you leave her, you may win or lose. // Unwillingly, I stayed there, as if I were an / impotent man being squeezed by an old woman."

According to historical sources, one reason for selecting the site chosen for Baghdad was because it was free of mosquitoes and had lots of fresh air, but after the city had been built, there were differing opinions from those who beheld the city and breathed its air. Tahir ibn al-Husayn al-Khuza'i (776–822) wrote: "People say, Your night, Oh Baghdad, / is lovely, the air cool and fresh. // By my life, your night is thus only / because the day is beset by hellish wind. // A slight comfort after great agony, / and people say at once: What a paradise!" And we have, as well, the testimony of Adam ibn 'Abd al-'Aziz al-Umawi (ninth century): "My night in Baghdad became longer; whoever spends a night in / Baghdad will stay awake, deprived of sleep. // As soon as day escapes, it becomes a land where mosquitoes / swarm, in pairs and alone. // Humming, their bellies white as if they were / pack mules repelled by spears." Ibn al-Mu'tazz describes his nights as follows: "Suffering at night, my eyelids still open; / sparks of fire sting my skin. // Birds blow in the ears, / full of blood, brimming."

In any event, Baghdad could not have achieved its supremacy without having been an industrial urban center from its earliest times. Its residents were known, for example, for their brilliance in building splendid boats and ships, some in special shapes, such as domes, lions, and eagles. According to extant statistics, there were thirty thousand of these ornate boats and ships; the Caliph al-Amin had a number of them. In his verses, Abu Nuwas (d. 813–5) described such ships: "God made mounted beasts submissive to al-Amin. / He had never made them obedient even for kings. // While the king's mounted beasts stride on the ground, / al-Amin passes on water, riding a forest lion."

Many verses refer to the rain as does that by Abu 'Abd Allah Ibrahim ibn Muhammad Niftawayhi (858–935): "Clouds water al-Karkh[46] with perpetual rain, / unceasingly falling, never stopping. // These abodes possess beauty and joy. / They have advantages over any other abode." Because the climate in Baghdad is dry, blessings or curses included in poems on the city and its dwellers frequently open with formulas such as "may God rain on Baghdad," "may the rain water the surface of your earth," "may He not rain on Baghdad," or "may clouds never rain upon you."

Poetry also chronicles spells when Baghdad was covered in snow and inspired poets. Ibn al-Mu'tazz described a sudden flurry of snow: "The clouds' eyes were bathed in water. / All at once they poured down snow, spreading it like white roses." Unlike Ibn al-Mu'tazz, al-Sharif al-Radi (930–77) had a different impression and makes an analogy between the damage caused by the snow and people's wickedness and evildoing:

> I see Baghdad, hit by snow,
> attacking early in the morning.

> As if the tips of her landmarks were burdened
>   she-camels
> with their skins removed.

> As if the snow were camels' saliva poured
> like a torrent, shot from a waterwheel.

It covered uplands, every valley;
upon its elevated spots a new white veil.

All valleys were smitten by snow;
all planes and uplands became dust colored.

Wherever you look from the hills,
you see only white; the consequence is only dark.

I say to the snow, as it hits
lands, more strongly or less:

Beware! Human minds are ice for any
generosity, favors are chilly.

If you want to pile up more miseries on the ones already
existing, you will never succeed.

Such analogy sounds familiar to me. For example, when a rare snow storm hit my own city, Haifa, in February 1950, it inspired different narratives by Jews and Palestinians in the political and cultural contexts of the city in the aftermath of the war of 1948.[47]

Due to neglect of the irrigation systems, floods were one of the most frequently chronicled natural catastrophes striking Baghdad as recorded by historians[48] and poets from the first centuries after its founding. For example, a flood in the year of 883 ruined seven thousand houses in al-Karkh. In 1243, 1248, 1255, and 1256 a series of floods ruined some of the city quarters, and in one case floods even entered the markets east of Baghdad. The city went on suffering from floods and in the twentieth century as Ma'ruf al-Rusafi (1875–1945) describes: "Flood's armies kept advancing. / They fell upon al-Karkh with a mighty uproar. // As they streamed onto houses with nauseous fluids, / the houses spat out their residents." Some tens of years later, Nazik al-Mala'ika (1923–2007) wrote: "Now the river has become a god. / Haven't our buildings washed their feet in its water? / It rises and pours its treasures in front of them. / It grants us mud and invisible death. / And now what is left for us? / Now, what has remained for us?"

As with any other urban center, Baghdad had intensified activities and busy squares, and poets had both a negative and positive view of them. According to Muti' ibn Iyas (704–85): "Time has increased evil and hardness — / it made us settle in Baghdad. // A town raining dust on people / as the sky pouring drizzle." And another anonymous poet writes: "Tell me, my friend, will God let me get out of Baghdad, / never again to set eyes on her palaces? // Never again to behold her square raising dust / whenever voices of mules and donkeys are heard?" Unlike these poets, Muhammad ibn 'Abd Allah al-Salami (947–1002) was inspired by the busy activities of the square: "I see a busy square, galloping horses / leading armored fighters. Nobody leads them. // Once I was riding for pleasure on a noble horse, / with a body but no heart. // Galloping on, I imagined the ground was a lady's face; / the Tigris was the eye, the horse, the eyeball." In the nineteenth century, city centers such as the city squares reflected Baghdad's situation. The square between the Ahmadi Mosque and the fortress of Baghdad was a dirty square where people used to gather to sell their merchandise and where animals and dogs used to wander. Then Ottoman ruler Mehmed Selim Sirri Pasha gave an order to clean it up and plant all kinds of trees there. The square bloomed; it became a garden full of flowers and aromatic plants. Ahmad al-Shawi (1844–99) wrote: "May Baghdad's square be a lesson for all, / as anyone who speaks the truth must admit."

In the early centuries after Baghdad's founding, scenes of the Tigris were frequently depicted together with the bridges which connected what were called Madinat al-Mansur and Madinat al-Mahdi, each on the other bank of the Tigris. The bridges that contributed to the development of Baghdad also served the city's residents as places for rest, contemplation, and wandering around and poets used to write poems about them. One favorite image was the moon upon the river. Ibn al-Tammar al-Wasiti (tenth century) writes, "Full moon sits in the western horizon as though / a golden bridge stretching between the two banks." Or as 'Ali ibn Muhammad al-Tanukhi (892–953) writes, "What a beautiful river when night falls! / The moon stirs westward toward the horizon. // The Tigris on the moon, a blue carpet; / the moon over the river, a golden veil." Sometimes the image of the moon shifts or blurs into other images; thus with the face of the young cupbearer at a wine party in Mansur ibn Kay-aghlagh's (d. 960) verses: "Many a night did I spend with her full moon / hovering over the Tigris before it disappeared. // The cupbearer passed around the wine; / I imagined he was a full moon bearing a star. // When the moon is about to set, it is / a golden sword unsheathed over the water." Another oft-used im-age was a bridge over the Tigris; thus 'Ali ibn al-Faraj al-Shafi'i (tenth century?) writes:

> How wonderful is the bridge, stretching over the Tigris, great in perfection, saturated with glamor and beauty.
>
> Glory and honor to Iraq, consolation and solace for gloomy lovers.
>
> Curiously, when approaching and fixing your eyes on it, you see a perfumed line written on parchment.
>
> Or an ivory with ebony decorations — elephants stepping on soil of mercury.

Almost one thousand years later, Ma'ruf al-Rusafi wrote, "As if al-Zawra' were a young woman, the bridge / on her thin waist like a belt. // Like a necklace of pearls on / the neck of the river. // Al-Rusafa longed for al-Karkh, / extending a hand to touch her." Reading the aforementioned verses about the Tigris and the bridges upon the river recalls William Wordsworth's lines "Composed upon Westminster Bridge, September 3, 1802": "Earth has not anything to show more fair; / Dull would he be of soul who could pass by / a sight so touching in its majesty. / This City now doth, like a garment, wear / The beauty of the morning; silent, bare."

Baghdad was the city of lovers, worldly and divine. As it was the greatest urban center of the Islamic empire, this is no wonder. Certain parts of the city provided opportunities for the intermingling of the sexes and had much more to offer than other smaller and less prominent spaces. "Oh crow of separation,"[49] says one agonized earthly anonymous lover, "why have you landed / in Baghdad to settle and never leave? Are you so salubrious?" // Tears fell from the crow's eyes, while replying: / We fulfill our desires and then leave. // Baghdad, you know, is a house of calamity. / May God save us from this very prison."

On the other hand, it is noteworthy that contrary to traditional thought where mystical phenomena thrives in isolated places such as deserts, mountains, and the countryside, Baghdad was one of the greatest centers of Muslim mysticism, namely, Sufism. Scholars even refer to a Baghdadi Sufi tendency, which places heavy stress on *zuhd* (asceticism) as opposed to the Khurasanian ecstatic tendency. Al-Husayn ibn Mansur al-Hallaj (858–922), whose mysticism was Khurasanian, spent his last period in Baghdad, where he was executed for having declared, "I am the Truth" — "Truth" being a synonym for God in mystical parlance. His divine love poems were inspired by Baghdadi scenes: "Oh breeze, please tell the gazelle that / water only increases thirst. // I have a lover; His love is ever inside me; / if He wishes to walk, He can do it on my cheeks. // His soul is mine — mine His; / if He wishes, I too wish; if I wish, He does too." Comparing the beloved with the gazelle is one of the traditional themes of Arabic love poetry. With its lovely body and large, soft eyes, the gazelle meant to the Arabs all that was beautiful in nature. Though Baghdad was always in the background, al-Hallaj yearned only for the divine: "I have no need for places, neither wide nor narrow. / I do not need any cities." Another lover of the divine, Muhyi al-Din ibn al-'Arabi (1165–1240), wrote: "Oh you, the ben-tree of the valley[50] / on Baghdad river's bank. // A melancholic dove on a swaying bough / filled me with grief."

There were poets who compared Baghdad to other cities, as did Abu Ishaq al-Sabi (925–94): "Alas, I deeply miss Baghdad; / I miss her snowy water. // Here, in ugly Basra, we are watered / with only sickly, yellowish drinks. // How could we be satisfied drinking it, while in our own land, / we clean our asses with purer water?!" Or Ibn al-'Arabi: "The most beloved of the cities of God, after Medina, / Mecca, and Jerusalem, is Baghdad." This particular "tradition of comparison" has lasted throughout Baghdad's history. While staying in Tibriz, Radi al-Qazwini (1819–68) wrote: "My beloved people in al-Zawra' of Iraq, / we have been apart for too long; when will we meet? // Tibriz is not a refuge for eloquent Arabic speakers. / Could you ever compare Turks to the Arabs of Iraq?" And Ahmad Shawqi (1868–1932) urged his readers: "Forget Rome and Athens and all that they contain. / All jewels are only in Baghdad. // At the mention of the Abode of Peace, the Abode of Law, Rome, / hastens to congratulate her. // When they meet, Rome cannot equal her in eloquence. / In a court of law, she cannot challenge her rival." These verses are from Shawqi's poem *Nahj al-Burda* (In the Manner of the Cloak), a tribute to the Prophet Muhammad. The poem is a *mu'arada* — an attempt to surpass an earlier poem by shaping a poem with the same meter and rhyme and on the same topic. In this case, Shawqi's poem is in competition to the earlier poem *al-Burda* (The Cloak), written by Sharaf ad-Din al-Busiri (1213–95).

Just as medieval Arabic poetry frequently referred to Baghdad, there were other literary writings such as the *maqamat* (literally, assemblies) that alluded to various dimensions of Baghdad and life in the city. The *maqamat* themselves are a type of rhymed prose writing, eloquent and ornate that characteristically lapse into verse. All great writers of this genre wrote *maqamat* set in Baghdad as did Badi' al-Zaman al-Hamadhani (969–1007), his twelfth *maqama* called *al-Maqama al-Baghdadhiyya (The Baghdadi Assembly)*, and another, his thirtieth *maqama*, called *al-Rusafiyya (The Rusafa Assembly);*[51] and Abu Muhammad al-Hariri (1054–1122), his thirteenth *maqama* called *al-Maqama al-Baghdadiyya (The Baghdadi Assembly)*,[52] and so on. Ibn al-Kazaruni (d. 1298) wrote a Baghdadi *maqama* that was not only set in Baghdad but also included descriptions of the city before its destruction by the Mongols with many *ubi sunt* exclamations ("Where are those who were before us?") to indicate nostalgia for the bygone wondrous city of Baghdad.[53]

Returning to the poetic output, we arrive at the aforementioned major event that poets chronicled in detail: the destruction of Baghdad in 1258. Hulagu (1217–65), the Mongol conqueror and founder of the Il-Khanid dynasty of Persia, launched a wave of conquests throughout the Islamic world. After direct control of much of the Islamic world south of the Oxus had slipped from the hands of the Mongols, Hulagu was entrusted by the Great Khan Mongke with the task of recovering and consolidating the Mongol conquests in western Asia. He overcame the resistance of the Isma'ilis of northern Persia, routed a caliphal army in Iraq, captured Baghdad, and murdered the Caliph al-Musta'sim (reigned 1242–58). His army sacked the city and the killing, looting, and burning lasted for several days. The number killed during the fifty-day siege was estimated to be between 800,000 and 1,300,000. According to some accounts, the Tigris and Euphrates ran red with the blood of scholars.[54] Most of the city's monuments were wrecked and burned, and the famous libraries of Baghdad, including the House of Wisdom, were eradicated. Poems and chronicles describe how copies of the Qur'an "became cattle's fodder." Books were used to make a passage across the Tigris: "The water of the river became black because of the ink of the books." Books were also pillaged from Baghdad's famous libraries and transported to a new library that Hulagu erected near Lake Urmiya.[55]

As a result of these events, Baghdad remained depopulated and in ruins for several centuries, and the event is conventionally regarded as the end of the Islamic golden age. The poetry of the times was a faithful mirror of those events that inspired as well many poets in the centuries following and up to our own times — Hulagu being taken as the figure of the archetypal cruel dictator. Taqi al-Din ibn Abi al-Yusr (1193–1273) wrote: "Oh visitors to al-Zawra', please do not come here. / Baghdad is no longer a refuge; no one is here anymore. // The crown of the caliphate, the great monuments, / all has been burned to ashes." Al-Majd al-Nashabi (d. 1259) complains that

> Heresy fanned a fire; Islam was burned,
> no hope of the fire being quenched.

> Oh grief, what a loss for the kingdom, for true religion,
> what a loss —Baghdad struck with misery.

> Death is touching me;
> death is doing what it wants.

> It is a dark cruel catastrophe
> which turns a child's hair and liver white.

The liver was viewed in ancient Arab culture as the seat of passion, especially that of burning feelings such as hate, spite, and malice. Standing in Abadan, Saʿdi Shirazi (1219–94), looked into the water of the Tigris, and seeing "red blood flowing to the sea," he started weeping: "I kept close my eyelids to prevent tears flowing; / when they overflowed, the dam could not stop them. // If only after the destruction, Baghdad's eastern breeze / had blown over my grave!" He described how women's honor in captivity was violated by the Mongols and how

> They ran barefoot from desert to desert;
> they were so tender, they could not walk on a bridge.

> By your life, had you seen them on the night of their
>   flight,
> it was as if virgins were stars falling into darkness.

> . . . A cry is heard: Oh lost sense of honor, help!
> But who would help a bird in a falcon's grip?

> They were led like sheep in the desert's midst,
> noble women unused to being chided.

> They were dragged away, their breasts raised, their faces
>   unveiled,
> driven out from their private abodes.

As with the civil war following the death of Harun al-Rashid, the events of 1258 were described as *mundus inversus,* such as in a poem by Shams al-Din Muhammad ibn 'Abd Allah al-Kufi (1226–1276): "Oh, what a catastrophe! No one saved himself from its / calamities; kings and slaves are equal." Shams al-Din Mahmud ibn Ahmad al-Hashimi al-Hanafi (thirteenth century) addresses the destroyed abode: "Oh house, where are your dwellers? / Where reside glory and honor? // Oh house, where are the days of your elegance and kindness, / when your slogans were greatness and respectfulness? // Oh house, by God, since your stars have set, / darkness has covered us after the light."

On the whole, all that was written about the destruction of Baghdad, both at the time and in the succeeding decades and centuries, reflects the paradigm that sees political changes as pivotal in their effects on the religious and cultural life. Hulagu has been engraved on the Arabs' memory as the fundamental reason for the destruction of their great medieval civilization and the cause for the cultural stagnation of the Arab world until the renaissance *(nahda)* in the nineteenth century. Arabs place emphasis, prompted by European orientalists, on the descriptions of the destructions of cultural institutions and libraries, the burning of books by the Mongol army, their throwing of books into the Tigris and using them as a bridge to cross the river, and the killing of many of the scholars and men of letters in Baghdad.[56] We find this not only in modern historical books but also in literary histories, and even in modern poetry and prose. Not a few modern Arab officials have used the Hulagu myth for their own aims as did, for example, the late Egyptian president Gamal 'Abd al-Nasir (1918–70). A well-known Swiss writer on Middle Eastern affairs even quotes "a high Syrian government official" as saying, "in deadly earnest," that "if the Mongols had not burnt the libraries of Baghdad in the thirteenth century, we Arabs would have had so much science that we would long since have invented the atomic bomb. The plundering of Baghdad put us back centuries."[57]

Bernard Lewis explains that this is an extreme, even a grotesque formulation, but the thesis that it embodies was developed by European scholars, who saw in the Mongol invasions "the final catastrophe which overwhelmed and ended the great Muslim civilization of the Middle Ages." This judgment of the Mongols "was gratefully, if sometimes surreptitiously, borrowed by romantic and apologetic historians in Middle Eastern countries as an explanation both of the ending of their golden age, and of their recent backwardness."[58] Yet, scholars now argue that this thesis is definitely unjustified as the signs of the stagnation had appeared long before Hulagu descended upon Baghdad. The successive "blows by which the Mongols hewed their way across western Asia, culminating in the sacking of Baghdad and the tragic extinction of the independent caliphate in 1258," as H. A. R. Gibb writes, "scarcely did more than give finality to a situation that had long been developing."[59] Even some modern Arab intellectuals and historians feel that the descriptions of the sacking of Baghdad as regards the cultural losses were much exaggerated. Constantine Zurayk comments that

> some of us still believe that the attacks of the Turks and the Mongols are what destroyed the Abbasid Caliphate and Arab power in general. But here also the fact is that the Arabs had been defeated internally before the Mongols defeated them and that, had those attacks been launched against them when they were in the period of growth and enlightenment, the Mongols would not have overcome them. On the contrary the attacks might have revitalized and re-energized them.[60]

In any event, since the destruction of Baghdad, Hulagu and the year of 1258 have become a metaphor for the decline of Arab-Muslim civilization and modern Arab poets have used his figure in order to allude to other catastrophes that have struck the Arab world. However, sometimes the figure of Hulagu is described in Arabic poetry positively, and that is to serve specific aims. For example, while spending a sabbatical year in the United States, the Palestinian poet Mishil Haddad (1919–96) missed his homeland and his town Nazareth. In his exile he was surrounded by books he perceived to be in opposition to the natural order of things. After returning to his natural environment in his homeland, he wrote the poem "The Books," using the stories about Hulagu's burning of the books in Baghdad. The books are used here as metonym for the disasters that sciences and rational thinking have brought to mankind: "Hulagu will come and burn the books, / Before eyes grow feeble, / Before ideas are muddled, / Before their crowded languages teach us / Tranquility, / Before that, / He will come!" It seems that Haddad was inspired by William Wordsworth's romantic dictum, "Up! up! my friend, and quit your books, / or surely you'll grow double. / Up! up! my friend, and clear your looks. / Why all this toil and trouble?"

But, in general, Hulagu's destruction is obviously described in terms of the demonic, his forces as "barbaric," similar to those forces that brought about the destruction of the Roman Empire. In other words, the Hulagu story has been united with the myth of the "anticivilization barbarians." In almost all modern poems written about the destruction of Baghdad by the Mongols there are intertextual dialogues with modern non-Arabic literary works that refer to the myth of the barbarians, the most famous of which are "Waiting for the Barbarians" (1904) by the Greek poet Constantine P. Cavafy (1863–1933) and the novel *Waiting for the Barbarians* (1983) by J. M. Coetzee (b. 1940).[61] The Egyptian poet Salah Abd al-Sabur (1931–81) concluded his poem "The Tatars Have Attacked" with the following: "We swear in hatred that tomorrow we will rejoice in the blood of the Tatars. / Oh Mother, please tell the children: / Dear children, / We will walk amongst our grey houses, when day rises / And build again what the Tatars destroyed." Sargon Boulus (1944–2007) used the metaphor of Hulagu in two poems in the present anthology; the first is "Hulagu Praises Himself":

I am Hulagu!
A sea of grass
crossed by horses in silence.
A sword hates having to wait in its sheath,
Beneath walls that dream of crows;
Walls, walls, the refugees see me
In their dreams amid the ruins;
Prisoners sharpen a small straw from my horse.

The second poem, "Hulagu (New Series)," which was published five years later, conducts a dialogue with the former: "Death speaks in my name: / 'I am Hulagu.' // A sword in its sheath, never resting. // Its shadow, wherever it throws itself / Begets a cloud of hungry eagles / Hovering over the houses."

In the next centuries after the city fell to the Mongols, Baghdad was pushed into the margins of the Arab and Islamic world. The Mamluk capital, Cairo, replaced her as the capital of the Muslim world, and for centuries the name of Baghdad was lost in Europe or confused with Babylon. After the invasion of Tamerlain (1401), al-Maqrizi wrote in 1437 that "Baghdad is but a heap of ruins; there is neither mosque, nor congregation, nor market place. Most of its waterways are dry, and we can hardly call it a town."[62] In 1534 Baghdad was captured by the Ottoman Turks, and under their rule Baghdad fell into a period of further decline. European travelers visiting the city during the sixteenth and seventeenth centuries reported that Baghdad was a center of commerce with a cosmopolitan and international atmosphere where three main languages (Arabic, Persian, and Turkish) were spoken — at the same time mentioning neglected quarters where many houses were in ruins. Sir Thomas Roe, the British ambassador at Constantinople from 1621 to 1628, confused Baghdad with Babylon. The French traveler Tavernier, describing his journey down the Tigris in 1651, related that he arrived at "Baghdad, qu'on appelle d'ordinaire Babylon."[63] Only after the French orientalist Antoine Galland translated the *Arabian Nights* into French did Europeans again take an interest in Baghdad.

In 1774, we find a report that "this is the grand mart for the produce of India and Persia, Constantinople, Aleppo and Damascus; in short it is the grand oriental depository." However, in the overall picture, Baghdad was in constant decline; in one report, its population was at a low of fifteen thousand. To think that during the tenth century its population was around a million and a half! The poet 'Abd al-Ghani al-Jamil (1780–1863) served as mufti of Baghdad in a period when the Ottoman ruler 'Ali Rida ruled with great cruelty and his soldiers behaved violently, abusing women and stealing money and gold from residents. Al-Jamil publicly resisted this behavior, writing poems not only against the oppressor, but also against the very Baghdadi people who suffered — for their indifference when the ruler's men had burned down their dwellings and library. He compared Baghdad of the past to contemporary Baghdad:

> My condolences for Baghdad, what a town!
> Once glory nested here; now, it has flown away.
>
> She was a bride like the morning's sun;
> her jewels were not to be lent.
>
> An abode for warrior lions,
> a sanctuary for frightened fugitives.
>
> Alas, no refuge now for the needy.
> Her people offer no shelter.
>
> The newcomers are blind,
> knowing not good from evil.
>
> While the lion disappears into the forest,
> The bull is now the chief master.
>
> Prosperous trade has perished;
> Baghdad is a present-day hell.
>
> On her fences owls perch wailing:
> What a wreck! What a wreck!

In 1816 Dawud Pasha arrived on the scene and brought a degree of prosperity. He maintained control over the tribes and restored order and security. He took care of the irrigation system, established factories, encouraged local industry, built bridges and mosques, founded three *madrassas,* organized an army of about twenty thousand, and had a French officer train it. However, he imposed heavy taxes, and after his fall along with floods and plagues, Baghdad still suffered from marginality. From 1831 to the end of the Ottoman period, Baghdad was directly under the rule of Constantinople, and some governors tried to introduce reforms.[64]

The activities of European travelers who visited Baghdad during the nineteenth century would prove to be significant. They brought to Baghdad the conception of Enlightenment, inspiring and pushing Baghdadis in the direction of modernization. Although these travelers came from a European society that viewed East/West and Arab/European as distinct categories, they were imbued with the Kantian conception of Enlightenment that presented its concepts in universal terms and spoke of "mankind's exit from its self-incurred immaturity." Kant saw immaturity as the inability to make use of one's own understanding without the guidance of another: "Self-incurred is this inability if its cause lies not in the lack of understanding but rather in the lack of the resolution and the courage to use it without the guidance of another. *Sapere aude!* Have the courage to use your own understanding! is thus the motto of enlightenment."[65] It is no coincidence that the Christian intellectual Butrus al-Bustani (1819–83) delivered in Beirut on February 15, 1859, "A Speech about the Culture of the Arabs,"[66] in which he expressed the Kantian conception. Al-Bustani referred to his fellow countrymen as the "generation of knowledge and light" and called upon them to wake up.

Under Midhat Pasha (governed 1869–72), the leading advocate of Ottoman *tanzimat* reforms, a modern *vilayet* system was introduced, Baghdad being one of the *vilayets*. In 1869 the first publishing house, the *vilayet* printing press, was established in Baghdad. The same year, Midhat Pasha founded *al-Zawra',* the first newspaper to appear in Iraq as the official organ of the provincial government; it was a weekly that lasted until March

1917. In 1870 he founded a tramway linking Baghdad with Kazimayn.[67] With the exception of a few French missionary schools and schools for minorities, there had been no modern schools in Baghdad, but between 1869 and 1871, Midhat Pasha established modern schools, a technical school, junior (Rushdi) and secondary (I'dadi) military schools, and junior and secondary civil (Mulki) schools.

Minorities in Baghdad enjoyed a rare tolerance for the times.[68] In 1846 Rabbi Israel-Joseph Benjamin II said that "nowhere else as in Baghdad have I found my coreligionists so completely free of that black anxiety, of that somber and taciturn mood that is the fruit of intolerance and persecution."[69] The Christian and Jewish communities became the pioneers in modern education. In 1864 the Alliance Israelite Universelle (AIU), a Jewish School, was founded in Baghdad.[70] It offered a predominantly secular education and had a Western cultural orientation. It was to play a major role in the modernization of the local educational system. Visiting Baghdad in 1878, Grattan Geary, editor of the *Times of India,* wrote that instruction in the AIU School was of the best modern kind: "Arabic is the mother tongue of the Baghdad Jews," but many of them speak and read English "with wonderful fluency," and also, "they speak French with singular purity of accent and expression."[71]

This was also the time when Baghdad started to regain its position as one of the great urban centers in the Middle East. The *Gazetteer of Baghdad* (compiled in 1889) mentioned in its chapter on the ethnography of the city that "the present population is now estimated at about 116,000 souls, or 26,000 families divided thus: Turks, or of Turkish descent, 30,000 souls; Persians 1,600; Jews 40,000; Christians 5,000; Kurds 4,000; Arabs 25,000; Nomad Arabs 10,000."[72] The population of the city was gradually increasing, and in 1904 it was estimated at about 140,000. According to the last official yearbook of the Baghdad *Vilayet* (1917), the population figures for the city were as follows: Arab, Turks, and other Muslims except Persians and

Kurds: 101,400; Persians 800; Kurds 8,000; Jews 80,000; Christians 12,000.[73] By 1918, the population was estimated to be 200,000.

Baghdad remained under Ottoman rule until 1917 when it was taken by the British during World War I. The aim of Faysal, who became King of Iraq on August 23, 1921, was to create "an independent strong Arab state, which will be a cornerstone for Arab unity."[74] Thus, the Iraqi constitution of March 21, 1925, stated that "there is no difference between the Iraqi people in rights before the law, even if they belong to different nationalities, religions and languages."[75] Expressions overtly inclusive of all citizens are not surprising since Arab nationalists from their earliest phases had considered non-Muslims living among the Arabs as part of the Arab "race." Travelers to Baghdad were impressed with the great admixture of ethnicities, the diversity of speech, the rare freedom enjoyed by non-Muslims, and the great tolerance among the masses. The free intermingling of peoples left its imprint on the dialects of Baghdad.

With the recognition of Iraq as an independent state, Baghdad had gradually regained some of its former prominence as a significant center of Arabic culture. This was a time when, on the political level, the relationship between the authorities in Baghdad and the West became a major issue, which is also reflected in poetry. For example, in a celebration held in 1929 by the National Party on the occasion of a visit to Baghdad by the rich American Mr. Craine, Ma'ruf al-Rusafi recited a poem in which he describes Iraq as "a prisoner of the West, / like a debtor to a creditor. // The East here, the West there — / deceived and deceiver." In fact, the British mandate from the League of Nations operated behind the facade of a native government in which every Iraqi minister had a British advisor. This was despite the fact that the entire Iraqi educational system at the time was harnessed to the ideas of Arabness and Arabization.[76] Sati' al-Husri (1880–1968), director general of education in Iraq (1923–27) and Arab nationalism's first true ideologue, argued that "every person who is related to the Arab lands and speaks Arabic is an Arab."[77] With the aim of making the mixed population of the new nation-state homogeneous and cohesive, he looked upon schools as the means by which to indoctrinate the young in the tenets of Pan-Arabism, seeking the "assimilation of diverse elements of the population into a homogenous whole tied by the bonds of specific language, history, and culture to a comprehensive but still exclusive ideology of Arabism."[78] The eloquent secularist dictum "Religion is for God, the fatherland is for everyone"[79] was in popular circulation. Qur'anic verses fostering religious tolerance and cultural pluralism, such as "No compulsion is there in religion"[80] and "To you your religion, and to me my religion!"[81] were often quoted. The Iraqi writer 'Aziz al-Hajj (b. 1926), who worked in the education system, saw the composition of his own class (1944–47) in the department of English at the High School for Teachers in Baghdad (Dar al-Mu'allimin al-'Aliya) as a significant and symbolic representation of the harmony among the religious communities of Baghdad: out of eight students, four were Jewish, including one female student; two were Christian; and two were Muslim. He wrote: "The coexistence and intermixing between the different communities and religious sects in Baghdad is exemplary."[82]

As an offspring of a family that emigrated from Baghdad to Israel at the beginning of the 1950s, I will take as an example the Jewish residents of Baghdad who played a major role in the life of the city during the first half of the twentieth century. In 1914 Baghdad was, numerically, "a greater Jewish than Muslim city with its law-abiding, Arabic-speaking Jewish community."[83] The Civil Administrative of Mesopotamia, in its annual review for the year 1920, stated that the Jews were "a very important section of the community, outnumbering the Sunnis or Shias."[84] According to Elie Kedourie (1926–92), "Baghdad at the time could be said to be as much a Jewish city as an Islamic one."[85] Jewish poets wrote about Baghdad even after the mass emigration of the Jews to Israel following its independence. The most famous of the Iraqi-Jewish poets was Anwar Sha'ul (1904–84), who started to publish during the 1920s under the pseudonym of Ibn al-Samaw'al (the son of al-Samaw'al), referring to the pre-Islamic Jewish poet al-Samaw'al ibn 'Adiya,' who was proverbial in Arabic ancient heritage for his loyalty. According to the ancient sources, al-Samaw'al refused to hand over weapons that had been entrusted to him. As a consequence, he would witness the murder of his own son by the Bedouin chieftain who laid siege to his fortress al-Ablaq in Tayma', north of Medina. He is commemorated in Arab history by the well-known saying "as faithful as al-Samaw'al." In one of his poems Sha'ul said: "Faithful I will stay like al-Samaw'al / whether happy in Baghdad or miserable." And in another poem: "My childhood blossomed by the waters of the Tigris. / The days of my youth drank of the Euphrates." Another prominent Iraqi-Jewish poet, Mir Basri (1911–2006), feeling that because of his Jewish faith, there were doubts regarding his faithfulness to his Iraqi homeland and the Arab nation, wrote: "Oh friends of life! Even as my death draws near, / please bury me in the safety of the wide land. // Near my ancestors who slept for ages / in Baghdad's soil — this is the beloved mother." And Murad Michael (1906–86), when he was only sixteen, wrote the following verses: "My soul is your ransom, Oh my fatherland! / Be at peace; do not be afraid of any trials! // Today, your soil is my abode; / tomorrow your soil will embrace my corpse. // Oh my fatherland! Oh my fatherland!" Likewise, another Jewish poet, Ibrahim Ovadia (1924–2006), even when he suffered from the persecution of the Iraqi authorities, never hesitated to declare: "I am the son of Baghdad, whenever you meet me. / I am the son of Baghdad, wherever you see me." More than sixty years after their departure from Baghdad, this city is still alive in the minds and hearts of the Iraqi Jewish immigrants now in Israel or elsewhere. The poets among them write about Baghdad in both Arabic and Hebrew. When Iraqi missiles hit various parts of Israel in 1991, the Iraqi-born Israeli Hebrew poet Ronny Someck (b. 1951) wrote a poem entitled "Baghdad, February 1991":

Along these bombed-out streets my baby carriage was
    pushed.
Babylonian girls pinched my cheeks and waved palm
    fronds
Over my fine blond hair.
What's left from then became very black.
Like Baghdad and
Like the baby carriage we moved from the shelter
During the days of waiting for another war.
Oh Tigris, Oh Euphrates — pet snakes in the first map
    of my life,
How did you shed your skin and become vipers?

    All major modern Arabic poets have referred to Baghdad in their poetry, and the emergence of modernist Arabic poetry accompanied the transformation of Baghdad as a physical and spatial entity into what El Janabi considers in his afterword to be "an easy metaphor for revival and eclipse — for what disintegrates into a lulling daylight!" This was also the time when different poetic forms dictated changes in the ways Baghdad was imagined and described. Until the mid-twentieth century, the basic poetic form of the poems written on Baghdad was the classical *qasida*. This was the same poetic form that was developed in pre-Islamic Arabia and perpetuated throughout Arabic literary history. The *qasida* is a structured ode maintaining a uniform meter and a single end rhyme that runs through the entire piece; the same rhyme also occurs at the end of the first hemistich (half-line) of the first verse.

    The central poetic conception of the so-called neoclassical poets emerging from the late nineteenth century had been basically the same: the *qasida* is the sacred form for poetry, and the relationship between the poet and his readers was like that between an orator and his audience. It is when we come to the late 1940s and the rise and development of *al-shi'r al-hurr*, Arabic "free verse," that we encounter significant deviation from classical metrics. While the new free verse succeeded in gaining some measure of canonical status, traditional poets and critics felt that this new poetry was in opposition to the accepted and ancient form of Arabic poetry they were used to. Based upon earlier experiments of Arab poets and influenced by English and French poetry, the essential concept of "free verse" entails reliance on the free repetition of the basic unit of conventional prosody — the use of an irregular number of a single foot (taf'ila), instead of a fixed number of feet. The poet varies the number of feet in a single line according to need. The new form was closely associated with the names of two Baghdadi poets, Nazik al-Mala'ika and Badr Shakir al-Sayyab (1926–64), both of whom are represented in the present anthology. More recent developments in Arabic poetry, especially the type of prose poem known as *qasidat al-nathr*, with its variant types and forms, have gradually pushed the "free verse" into the margins.

The change in the poetry written about Baghdad since the 1960s demonstrates that modernity has taken hold and Arabic modernist poets are to a certain extent mainstream poets. The poets born of this decade — that is, their creativity became active in the sixties — are called the "generation of the sixties."[86] Instead of tribal membership, writes Abdul Kader El Janabi, "poets now felt that they belonged to a world-wide avant-garde. Baghdad figured as a metropolis, a state of mind, an explosive consonant." They no longer wrote "poetry about Baghdad; they wrote poetry of Baghdad. In the first instance, poets tinkled their bells in order that nostalgia be remembered, while in the second instance, poets nibbled the sun's black teat in order to set the limpid substance of the city ablaze and wave to the magnet of time!"

During the last three decades, Baghdad has suffered severe infrastructural damage, particularly following the First Gulf War, the Second Gulf War, the American-led occupation in 2003, and the sectarian violence and terrorist attacks. Nevertheless, the present population of Baghdad is now over seven million, making it the second largest city in the Arab world after Cairo. Almost all poems written about Baghdad during the last decades are melancholic and reflect the political and moral collapse in the reality of existence in the city, though the ethos of the city as a metaphor for Arabism and Islam still clings, and poets combine the reality of immediate history with the city's ethos. There are dialogues between modern and medieval poets. 'Abd al-Wahhab al-Bayyati (1926–99), for example, referred to al-'Abbas ibn al-Ahnaf's life and poetry: "Baghdad's taverns have darkened. / There is no use! / Al-'Abbas is dying of love." On the other hand, Sargon Boulus revived the figure of Sa'di Shirazi in his poem "In the Garden of Sa'di Shirazi (When He Was in Prison)." Buland al-Haydari (1926–96) in his turn wrote about the dictatorship in Baghdad at the time of Saddam Husayn, using the myth of Troy: "Troy died because of a wound inside us, because of a wound inside her, / Because of a blind silence that tied her children's tongues. / Troy, the silence killed her. / We have nothing inside her; she has nothing inside us save death, / Nothing but the corpse and the nail." In a later version of the poem, the poet substituted Baghdad for Troy throughout the poem. And Sargon Boulus follows from this with: "Oh Hangman, / Please return to your small village. / Today, we have expelled you and cancelled your job." In another poem, "I Have Come to You from There," Boulus described a chilling encounter with one of the victims who revisited him after death.

One of the major contemporary Arabic poets whose poetry about Baghdad reflects the new poetic change in Arabic poetry and at the same time expresses the influence of that change on the new attitude toward Baghdad — is not Baghdadi. He is not even Iraqi; moreover, he visited Baghdad only once. This is the Syro-Lebanese poet 'Ali Ahmad Sa'id, known by his pseudonym Adonis (b. 1930), whose poetry has been accompanying the city of Baghdad throughout the last fifty years. In 1961 Adonis, who at the time thought of himself as the new prophet of the utopian Baghdad, published his poem "Elegy for al-Hallaj" in which he orchestrates a dialogue with the poet-mystic al-Husayn ibn Mansur al-Hallaj (who lived in Baghdad more than a thousand years before). The speaker in the poem addresses al-Hallaj:

Your poisonous green quill,
Your quill, its veins swelled with flame,
With the rising star from Baghdad,
All are our history and prompt beginning,
In our land — in our recurring death.

Time laid itself on your hands.
The fire in your eyes
Swept away and spread to the sky.

Oh star rising from Baghdad,
Loaded with poetry and birth,
Oh poisonous green quill.

The flame alludes to the burning rage and connotes hope for the future of metaphorical Baghdad and likewise the quill that contains the star. Baghdad, the place where al-Hallaj was executed in 922, symbolizes the glories of ancient Arab and Muslim civilization. The star is rising from, and not over, Baghdad, in other words, there is an allusion to a possible universal message. The use of the active participle stresses the present relevance of the poem: the star *is rising now,* which is to say, the beginning of the 1960s. The spatial and temporal context of the poem is evident not only from the fact that the poem was published in the 1960s, in Arabic, and for Arab readers, but also from wording such as "the rising star from Baghdad," "our history," "our land," and "our recurring death." The very choice of the figure of al-Hallaj as the symbol of death and rebirth indicates the intention of the poet to stress the Arab and Islamic context of the poem as well as that of the entire collection in which it appears. Supposedly, according to its title, a lamentation for a Baghdadi personage who died more than a thousand years ago, "Elegy for al-Hallaj" is ironically transformed in the process of reading into a vision of the Arab nation's rebirth. Since the star is rising now, from Baghdad, the death of al-Hallaj is the bridge that Arab-Islamic civilization crosses to reach a more perfect existence.[87]

However, hopes and expectations for Baghdad as a symbol of Arab rebirth soon completely collapsed. Perhaps the most famous poetic text with this desperate message was written by Adonis in 1969; it was published only in May 2003 with the title: "Please, Look How the Dictator's Sword Is Sharpened, How Necks Are Prepared to Be Cut." It was published again in 2008 with the new title: "Poetry Presses Her Lips to Baghdad's Breast." Adonis wrote his lengthy outcry after visiting Baghdad in 1969, in fact his only visit to the city. He had gone as a member of the Lebanese Association of Writers' delegation and stayed in Baghdad for several days; then, returning to Beirut, he described Baghdad's cultural and political atmosphere of fear and death. At the beginning of the poet's description, the atmosphere in Baghdad is plainly established:

> Light in Baghdad is less shiny today than yesterday
>   when I arrived.
> Can light get flabby, as well?
> — Whisper, please! Every star here plans to kill its
>   neighbor.
> — Whisper? You mean as if I'm talking with death?
>
> Men turn their faces toward shapes. Shapes without
>   faces. Shapes like holes on the page of space.
> Men walk in the streets as if digging them. It seems to
>   me their steps have the forms of graves.

These lines and others may call to the mind sections of Orhan Pamuk's *Istanbul* where he describes the empty city as mirroring the empty souls, the "living dead," the corpse "that still breathes," and the feeling that expresses "the sadness that a century of defeat and poverty would bring to the people of Istanbul."[88] Like Pamuk, Adonis describes the "sewage systems, in open air, facing stores. Bad smells plunder the empty space ... embracing even the birds that revolt against him." But the resemblance is only superficial because Pamuk's sadness is in essence melancholic and the romantic sadness of a lover, "The Melancholy of Autumn,"[89] while Adonis's feeling is the sadness of a terrorized people. Adonis describes the fear among people when informants could be anyone — a neighbor, a friend, a relative or family member, or just a passerby. It is the atmosphere of an upside-down society. The poet does not see any difference between the Baghdad of 1258, the year Hulagu destroyed Baghdad, and the Baghdad of 1969, the year of his own visit: "The first, the Mongols destroyed; the second, / her children do the same." The speaker addresses Gilgamesh and accuses him of deluding the people that life has a secret to be revealed while in reality "life here is nothing but continuous death. Please, look how the dictator's sword is sharpened, how necks are prepared to be cut." Adonis does not hesitate to reject comparisons of Baghdad to paradise, some of which are quoted above: "Baghdad is a paradise? / Man is a paradise, not the place." He concludes with the following:

> And I saw how it happened that language was trans-
> formed into a huge army of predatory beasts. Until
> that moment in 1969, I had tried hard to distinguish
> between human beings, demons, and gods, while
> watching "the men of power in Iraq." Perhaps, that is
> why in Baghdad, when I was in the arms of the sun, I
> didn't feel anything other than absolute cold.
> But I can still say:
> Oh poetry, please press your lips to Baghdad's breast!

Some days before the American invasion of Baghdad in April 2003, Adonis wrote the poem "Salute to Baghdad," opening thus:

> Put your coffee aside and drink something else.
> Listening to what the invaders are declaring:
> "With the help of God,
> We are conducting a preventive war,
> Transporting the water of life
> From the banks of the Hudson and Thames
> To flow in the Tigris and Euphrates."

The poem concludes:

> A homeland almost forgets its name.
> Why?

A red flower teaches me how to sleep
In the laps of Damascus.
The fighter eats the bread of the song.
Don't ask, Oh poet, for nothing but disobedience
Will awake this land.

In another text, "Time Crushes into Baghdad's Body" written in 2005, Adonis contemplates the history of Baghdad against the background of her tragic present:

But, behold the river of history, how it flows into the
language plain, emerging from Baghdad's wounds. A
history that flies in my imagination as though it were
a black crocodile.
Except for the stars, does anyone know where Baghdad
is and where the Arabs are?
Behold! Here Time crushes into Baghdad's body. Her
tears have no kin but exile.

Oh Baghdad, in order to know you, do we have
to separate
Your names from their meanings?

Many poets have described the tragedy of Baghdad and its residents after the American occupation. In his poem "Baghdad, Don't Be in Pain!," the Egyptian poet Faruq Juwayda (b. 1945) illustrates the tragedy through the eyes of Baghdad's children: "Children in grieved Baghdad wonder / For what crime they are being killed, staggering on the splinters of hunger, / They share death's bread, then they bid farewell." Juwayda's poem was set to music and performed by the Iraqi singer Kazim al-Sahir (b. 1957) and became very popular.[90] Bushra al-Bustani (b. 1950), in her "A Sorrowful Melody," describes the horrors of the occupation: "The tanks of malice wander. / My wound / Is turned away like an abandoned horse / Scorched by an Arabian sun, / Chewed by worms. / Picasso paints another Guernica, / Painting Baghdad under the feet of boors." And there is the nostalgic Baghdad following the destruction: Sargon Boulus wrote "An Elegy for al-Sindibad Cinema," and Sinan

Antoon (b. 1967) wrote "A Letter to al-Mutanabbi (Street)" —
this street was the cultural heart of the city. On March 5, 2007,
after a suicide bombing had destroyed many bookshops and
killed twenty-six people, he wrote: "This is another chapter / In
the saga of blood and ink."

A study of poems and epigrams included in the *Palatine
Anthology* about Greek cities reaches the conclusion that the
vast majority of them "are laments for a fallen city, destroyed by
war, by nature, or the ravages of times. Others celebrate mythol-
ogy of a site."[91] Retrospectively, readers of the present anthology
might well arrive at similar conclusions in regard to Baghdad.
The utopian city of Harun al-Rashid, the realm of the *One
Thousand and One Nights* inclusive, was in the end a fallen city,
destroyed by wars and calamities. As in the case of Greek cit-
ies, immediately after its founding, many poems celebrated
the mythical city and its ethos as an Arab and Islamic city.
Even before the ravages of the second half of the twentieth
century, events had made reality more prominent than the ro-
mance, and people "brought reports eloquent of disillusion-
ment," as Reuben Levy testified to in his *A Baghdad Chronicle*
(1929).[92]

Thus, as seen above, the history of Baghdad may be divided
roughly into three periods: a) from its founding to its destruc-
tion by the Mongols (762–1258) — the city as the prestigious capi-
tal of the Islamic empire; b) from then to the establishment of
modern Iraq (1258–1921) — and continuous decline and decay;
and c) the present period with its glimpses of flowering and
thriving (such as those seen during the 1920s–1930s), which have
been buried under the ruins of decades of dictatorship and in-
ternal and external devastation.

In the beginning of his book *Baghdad: The City of Peace*
(1927), Richard Coke writes that the story of Baghdad is largely
the story of continuous war, and "where there is not war, there is
pestilence, famine and civil disturbance. Such is the paradox
which cynical history has written across the high aims implied
in the name bestowed upon the city by her founder."[93] More

than eighty-five years later, one cannot maintain that Coke was wrong in his historical judgment of Baghdad. In other words, the glorious Baghdad is only an image and memory of the remote past; the Baghdad of the present evokes only sadness, distress, and nostalgia for bygone days.

The writer and journalist Hussain al-Mozany (b. 1954), who currently lives in Berlin, wrote about the contrast between the Baghdad he left and the one he found after thirty years of absence, which "has become a non place, represented by concrete walls." Al-Rashid street "that some used to call Iraq's aorta, has committed suicide, and now all that is left is its long corpse stretched out along the scattered, blackened shops that mourn a street which bid its people farewell and then killed itself."[94] The poem "In Baghdad, Where My Past Generation Would Be" by Abdul Kader El Janabi (b. 1944) encapsulates all that lovers of Baghdad must feel nowadays:

> Where are you, my first years,
> Years of streets and cafés,
> Years of days and long walks,
> In the course of revolts with no pricking of conscience?
> Where are you, my first years?
> Oh my city, feverish with floods of memory,
> Where are you in that drawn stream?

Notes

1. Levy 1977 [1929], p. 1.

2. Abu-Lughod 1987, pp. 172–73.

3. Ibn al-Fuwati 2008, p. 72.

4. On place as an image of self in classical Arabic literature, see Hämeen-Anttila 2008, pp. 25–38.

5. Johnston 1984, p. xv.

6. Bell and de-Shalit 2011, p. 2.

7. It seems that Benjamin Disraeli tried to define the ethos of some cities when he said that "a great city, whose image dwells in the memory of man, is the type of some great idea. Rome represents conquest; Faith hovers over the towers of Jerusalem; and Athens embodies the pre-eminent quality of the antique world, Art."

8. On this controversy, see Lapidus 1969; Hourani and Stern 1970, mainly the introduction on pp. 9–24; Eickelman 1974, pp. 274–94; Serjeant 1980; Abu-Lughod 1987, pp. 155–76; Raymond 1994, pp. 3–18 (Raymond quotes, as well, a lecture given by Eugen Wirth in 1982, in which he suggested renouncing the term "Islamic city" in favor of the more general "Oriental city" since "Islam seems to be more inhabit-ant or occupant of Middle Eastern urban systems than the architect" [p. 12]); Khan 2008, pp. 1035–62.

9. Yaqut 1990, I, p. 541.

10. Khalis 2005, p. 8.

11. Al-Khatib al-Baghdadi 1931, p. 45; Yaqut 1990, I, p. 548; Ibn al-Fuwati 2008, p. 74; al-Alusi 1987, p. 18; Khalis 2005, p. 7.

12. Al-Khatib al-Baghdadi 1931, p. 119; Khalis 2005, pp. 8–9.

13. According to historical sources, al-Mansur laid the first brick for the city and recited the following Qur'anic text: "Surely the earth is God's and He bequeaths it to whom He will among his servants. The issue ultimate is to the godfearing" (al-A'raf [The Battlements], 127; translation according to Arberry 1979 [1964]), pp. 157–58. See Yaqut 1990, I, p. 543). For English references on the foundation of Baghdad

and its development, see Coke 1935 [1927], pp. 34–47; El-Ali 1970, pp. 87–101; Lassner 1970, pp. 103–18; Duri 1980, pp. 52–65; Duri 2012.

14. According to some sources, the city was called "The City of Peace" because one of the ninety-nine names of God is *al-Salam* and the intended meaning was "The City of God." Another suggestion is that the Tigris valley was called *Wadi al-Salam* (Valley of Peace) (Yaqut 1990, I, pp. 541–42).

15. *Yunus* (Jonah), 25–26; translation according to Arberry 1979 [1964], p. 200.

16. There are additional versions of the name, such as *Baghdadh, Baghdan, Maghdad, Maghdadh,* and *Maghdan* (Yaqut 1990, I, p. 541).

17. One explanation is that the city took the name from the Tigris, which was bent as it passed by the city (Le Strange 1900, p. 11).

18. Lapidus 2002, p. 56.

19. Ibn al-Fuwati 2008, p. 73; al-Alusi 1987, p. 13.

20. Al-Alusi 1987, p. 13.

21. Ibn al-Fuwati 2008, p. 74; al-Alusi 1987, p. 13.

22. Al-Alusi 1987, p. 13.

23. Yaqut 1990, I, p. 547; Ibn al-Fuwati 2008, p. 72; al-Alusi 1987, p. 22.

24. Yaqut 1990, I, p. 547; al-Alusi 1987, p. 22.

25. Al-Alusi 1987, p. 22.

26. Yaqut 1990, I, p. 547; al-Alusi 1987, p. 22.

27. Saba' (Sheba), 15; translation according to Arberry 1979 [1964], p. 439.

28. Al-Alusi 1987, p. 14.

29. Yaqut 1990, I, p. 547; al-Alusi 1987, p. 21.

30. Khalis 2005, p. 7.

31. Al-Dhahabi 1988–2004, p. 383. For another version of this episode, see Ibn Taghribirdi 1930, II, p. 29 (edition 1992, II, 36–37); on the liberal cultural atmosphere at the time, see also Yaqut 1990, III, pp. 242–44.

32. See Snir 1994b, pp. 51–75.

33. Coke 1935 [1927], p. 63; Ali 2010, p. 221; Toorawa 2005, pp. 13–15.

34. Eco 1984, p. 35. In Eco's novel, the historical background of fourteenth-century Christian Europe is reconstructed, but, at least

according to the myth of Hulagu, Baghdad's libraries had been destroyed in 1258 and Baghdad lost its cultural dominance in the Arab world before the events of the novel took place (see below).

35. Wasserstrom 1995, pp. 19–20.

36. On this number and the various calculations that enable scholars to reach it, see Micheau 2008, pp. 234–35.

37. Duri 1980, p. 64.

38. Dougherty 1980, p. x. Cf. Johnston 1984, p. xx.

39. The saying *al-shi'r diwan al-'Arab* is found in different forms in various medieval works, for example, Ibn Qutayba 1928, II, p. 185; al-Suyuti n.d., II, p. 470. Cf. Lyall 1930, p. xv. For an examination of the above saying with regard to the change in perception of poetry and its function during the emergence of Arabic-Islamic society, see Ouyang 1997, pp. 56–60.

40. Ibn Rashiq al-Qayrawani 1963, p. 65; al-Suyuti n.d., II, p. 473. The translation is according to Lyall 1930 with minor modifications.

41. See al-Alusi 1987, pp. 55–59; Matlub 1994, pp. 67–70.

42. Al-Karkh was known for being a place where people could visit and enjoy some rest and relaxation. Bordering al-Karkh's Gate was an artificial pond, Birkat Zalzal. It was named after Zalzal who had risen to fame and become known as "Zalzal the Player" by playing the *oud* for the Caliphs al-Mahdi, al-Hadi, and Harun al-Rashid. The beautiful young women gathering near al-Karkh's Gate and Birkat Zalzal inspired poets. 'Ali ibn al-Jahm composed these verses when he saw al-Mufaddal's slave girls there.

43. Ibn al-Jahm 1981, pp. 141–8; al-Alusi 1987, pp. 50–2. In the present book, I translated only the elegiac prelude *(nasib)*. For a complete translation of the poem, see Ali 2010, pp. 88–92, who relied on "version 3" of the poem (Ibn al-Jahm 1981, pp. 252–5). See also Stetkevych 1993, pp. 108–9.

44. When the city was founded, al-Mansur asked his son al-Mahdi to build the cantonment of Baghdad on the eastern shore of the Tigris. Later on, when al-Mahdi became the Caliph (reigned 775–85), he would build a quarter named al-Rusafa as part of Baghdad (Yaqut 1990, III, p. 53).

45. The translation of *'uyun al-maha* as "does' eyes" is based on Stetkevych 1993, p. 108; Ali 2010, p. 92 (who translated in the singular "doe's eyes").

46. A quarter on the western shore of the Tigris which runs through Baghdad.

47. See Rabinowitz and Mansour 2011, pp. 119–48.

48. See Micheau 2008, pp. 240–41.

49. The black crow, the "crow of separation" *(ghurab al-bayn),* is a frequent motif in Arabic poetry. The crow was looked upon as a bird of ill omen, and its caw was believed to bode the separation of lovers.

50. The ben-tree *(ban),* according to the poet, is the tree of light.

51. Al-Hamadhani 1983, pp. 55–59, 157–65; al-Hamadhani 1973, pp. 61–64, 122–28. *Baghdadh* is another version of the name of Baghdad. It appears as such in order to rhyme with *azadh* (dates) in the first line of the *maqama.*

52. Al-Hariri 1985, pp. 105–11; al-Hariri, 1969 [1867], pp. 176–81; al-Hariri 1980, pp. 54–57.

53. Hämeen-Anttila 2002, pp. 329–30; al-Alusi 1987, pp. 150–53.

54. Boyle 1968, pp. 348–49; Boswerth 1967, pp. 149–51; Muir 1924, pp. 591–92.

55. Hitti 1946, p. 378; Sedillot 1877, p. 293.

56. See, for example, D'Ohsson 1834–35, I, p. 387, as quoted by Browne 1951, II, p. 427; Nicholson 1956, p. 129; Goldziher 1966, p. 141. Cf. Browne 1951, II, p. 463.

57. Hottinger 1957 (as cited by Lewis 1973, p. 179). After the destruction of Baghdad, another myth developed: that of the Shiite treachery according to which two Shiite figures, the Vizier Ibn al-'Alqami (1197–1258) and the philosopher Nasir al-Din al-Tusi (1201–74), acted in the service of the Mongols. However, this myth hardly appears in Arabic poetry.

58. Lewis 1973, p. 179.

59. Gibb 1963, p. 141. Cf. Lewis 1973, pp. 179–98; Lewis 1968, p. 12; Wiet 1966, p. 243; Smith 1963, p. 40.

60. Zurayk 1956, p. 48. Cf. Von Grunebaum 1962, p. 255; Lewis 1973, p. 182.

61. On this myth and the intertextual dialog of these two literary works with a poem by the Palestinian Mahmud Darwish (1941–2008), see Snir 2008, pp. 123–66.

62. Raymond 2002, p. 18

63. Levy 1977 [1929], p. 9; Le Strange 1900, p. 348.

64. Duri 2012.

65. Kant 1996, pp. 58–64. The quotation is from page 58. For the original text, see Hinske 1973, pp. 452–65.

66. Al-Bustani 1859. On this speech and its importance, see Sheehi 2004, pp. 19–45; Abu-Lughod 1963, pp. 135–36.

67. Unlike most historians, some Iraqi scholars argue that Midhat Pasha's projects in Iraq did not have a positive outcome; see, for example, al-Wardi 1971, II, pp. 235–65.

68. Batatu 1978, p. 257 and the references in note 184.

69. Benjamin II 1856, p. 84.

70. For the role AIU played in the field of Jewish education in the Middle East, see Cohen 1973, pp. 105–56.

71. Geary 1878, I, pp. 132–33.

72. *Gazetteer of Baghdad, Compiled (under the orders of the Quarter Master General in India) for Political and Military Reference, 1889, by J. A. Barlow, A. Howlett, S. H. Godfrey* (Reprint by the General Staff, India, 1915), p. 3.

73. Quoted in the *Arab Bulletin,* no. 66, October 21, 1917.

74. Al-'Afif 2008, p. 65.

75. For the text of the constitution, see al-Husni 1974, I, pp. 319–34; the quotation is from p. 319.

76. Tibawi 1972, pp. 94–95.

77. Al-Husri 1965 [1955], p. 12.

78. Cleveland 1971, p. 63.

79. The slogan was probably coined by the Copt intellectual Tawfiq Dus in the Coptic congress in Asyut; see Carter 1986, pp. 290, 304, n. 2.

80. See *al-Baqara* (The Cow), 256; translation according to Arberry 1979 [1964], p. 37.

81. See *al-Kafirun* (The Unbelievers), 6; translation according to Arberry 1979 [1964], p. 664.

82. Al-Hajj 1999, pp. 125–31.

83. Longrigg and Stoakes 1958, p. 29.

84. Rejwan 1985, p. 210.

85. Kedourie 1989, p. 21.

86. See al-ʿAzzawi 1997.

87. On the poem, see Snir 1994a, pp. 245–56; Snir 2006c, pp. 117–30.

88. Pamuk 2006, pp. 253, 317.

89. The title of a chapter in Pamuk's *The Museum of Innocence* (Pamuk 2009, pp. 197–204).

90. http://www.youtube.com/watch?v=WVllUDZeedk.

91. Hartigan 1979, p. 102. *Palatine Anthology* is a collection of Greek poems and epigrams from 300 B.C. until A.D. 600.

92. Levy 1977 [1929]), p. 1.

93. Coke 1935 [1927], p. 15.

94. Al-Mozany 2010, pp. 6–19; Duclos 2012, pp. 399–400.

Muti' ibn Iyas (704–85)

[*Stars Whirling in the Dark*]

It was morning in Baghdad, we were carousing,
stirred by a white face and deep-black eyes.

In a house where glasses are akin
to stars whirling in the dark among drinking companions.

Our cupbearer mixed wine or served it pure;
what a wonderful wine when mixed!

Saffron powder was sprinkled over us,
above our heads crowns of golden jasmine.

I was still drinking when sunset arrived,
between melodies of castanets and lute.

[*Raindrops of Dust*]

Time has increased evil and hardness —
it made us settle in Baghdad.

A town raining dust on people
as the sky pouring drizzle.

May God destroy her soon as He wiped out
Kalwadha[1] because of the deeds of her inhabitants.

---

1. A village to the south of Baghdad that was destroyed toward the end of the Abbasid period.

'Abd Allah ibn al-Mubarak (736–97)

[*The Pious Ascetic in Baghdad*]

Please tell those preferring abstinence,
tell all considered to be pious:

Stay on the frontier, be modest;
Baghdad is not an abode for hermits.

Baghdad is a place only for kings,
an abode solely for hunters and knights.

Anon.

[Paradise Lost]

My God make rain fall upon Baghdad — what a paradise!
A pleasure for souls!

Alas, only for the wealthy is it a dream.
For the penniless, it is a heart-rending loss.

Anon.

[*House of Calamity*]

Oh crow of separation,[2] why have you landed
in Baghdad to settle and never leave? Are you so
    salubrious?

Tears fell from the crow's eyes, as he replied:
We fulfill our desires and then leave.

Baghdad, you know, is a house of calamity.
May God save us from this very prison.

———

2. The "crow of separation" (*ghurab al-bayn*).

Anon.

[*Men's Souls Are Sick*]

Day and night, I imagine the Arab land draw near,
even as I am further from Najd[3] and from its people too.

Baghdad is a mere despicable land,
though life there has its comforts.

It is a land where men's souls are sick,
the stench even stronger when it rains.

---

3. Najd (literally, highland) is the central region of the Arabian peninsula.

Anon.

[*I Am Leaving*]

Enough of moaning, thank God.
I could not manage in Baghdad anymore.

I consort with people who afford me no pleasure.
I keep company with people I deem undesirable.

I have not stayed in Baghdad for love of her people,
nor for need of anyone.

I am leaving; I despise her leaders.
I am abandoning her, bored and weary.

If calamities make me need them,
then let a donkey's dick screw the mother of calamity!

Anon.

[*Mean as They Are*]

May God rain on Baghdad; may He protect her;
alas, may the clouds not provide rain for her residents.

Mean as they are, amazingly so,
for goodness sake, why have they been allowed such a
    paradise?

Anon.

[*Ornamented Rhetoric and Lies*]

I abhor Baghdad; I abhor life there.
This is from experience, after a taste.

Baghdad's residents have no pity for the needy,
no remedy for the gloomy.

Whoever wishes to live among them
needs three things apart from an ability to reproach:

Korah's wealth in hand,
Noah's longevity, and Job's patience.

People whose encounters are embroidered
with ornamented rhetoric and lies.

Abandoning the path of nobility,
they rival each other instead in disobedience and
     sinfulness.

[Comparison]

One of the gardens of al-Hazn[4] or any part
of the village, barren and unplowed,

Is sweeter and more beautiful to my eye, when I pass by,
than Baghdad's al-Karkh[5] for all its pomegranate and
    blueberry.

---

4. A place near Baghdad.

5. A quarter on the western shore of the Tigris, which runs through
Baghdad.

Anon.

[*Never Again*]

Tell me, my friend, will God let me get out of Baghdad,
never again to set eyes on her palaces?

Never again to behold her square raising dust,
whenever voices of mules and donkeys are heard?

al-ʿAbbas ibn al-Ahnaf (750–809)

[Oh Sun of Baghdad!]

Oh, sun of Baghdad! I am sick;
your friendship and tenderness have passed away.

I fell in love with the sun — who has ever seen a man
in love with a sun?

When I did not get your letters,
as was usual when we were beloved, I said:

I wish the wind would run fast,
frequently fulfilling our wishes.

My heart, though made miserable,
never concealed its beat and throbbing;

Raving about a tender and splendid gazelle,
the lips are black, dressed with a cloth of beauty;

A naive gazelle decorated with earring,
no, in fact, the gazelle decorates the ring;

Beauty and glamor obeyed her,
amazing, of itself, she behaves arrogantly;

But Fate prevented seeing her,
I wish Fate would be ruined.

Oh moon, dusk escaped from you;
Oh pearl that the shell cannot shelter.

Oh paradise, whose residents never die,
all hearts to you hurry.

[*From Harun al-Rashid's Mouth*]⁶

The three young ladies possessed me,
occupied every space of my heart.

Please, let me know: How all people obey me,
and here I obey and they resist?

Their powerful authority of love, it seems,
stronger than my authority.

[*The Eye's Greatest Delight*]

We stayed in Baghdad against our will,
when we had become acquainted with her, we left
    involuntarily.

Loving lands is not our habit;
the bitterest in life is to leave people you love.

I left her though she was the eye's greatest delight;
I left my heart there hostage.

---

6. It was usual for poets to recite verses as if they were Harun al-Rashid.

Harun al-Rashid (763–809)

[I Will Not Forgive Myself][7]

Peace be upon the far-off emigrant;
the sad lover sends you his greetings.

A gazelle whose pasture was between al-Balikh,[8]
Dayr Zakka,[9] and Baghdad's wooden bridge.

Oh he who ill-treats himself,
leaving behind his beloved.

I will forgive my beloved, forgiveness is my nature,
I will not forgive myself.

---

7. In 796 Harun moved his court and the governmental offices from Baghdad to al-Raqqa in the mid-Euphrates region and spent most of his reign there. Occasionally he would spend time in Baghdad.

8. A river in al-Raqqa.

9. A village in the green agricultural belt surrounding the city of Damascus in the South and East.

Shamsa (eighth century)

[*Separation*][10]

By God, I didn't leave you due to my fortitude,
but because of my strong love.

Many secrets I shared with my heart;
I never uttered them when I met you.

---

10. Shamsa was a slave girl who used to play the *tunbur* (a sort of mandolin) and to sing for Harun al-Rashid. These verses were written on her headband.

Anon.

[I Weep Blood][11]

I weep blood over Baghdad,
I lost the comfort of an elegant life.

Anxiety has replaced happiness;
instead of prosperity, there is only misery.

Enviers' eyes have smitten her;
their ballistas have exterminated Baghdad's residents.

People were violently thrown into fire;
a woman mourned her drowned dearest.

Another woman yelled: What a dreadful morning!
She was weeping for her lost brother.

A woman with the eyes of a gazelle, full of tears, a coy lady,
her shirts smeared with perfume;

Escaping fire, she was straightaway raped, before
her father's eyes; at once he desperately jumped into the
    fire.

---

11. Harun al-Rashid virtually dismembered the empire by apportioning it
between his two sons al-Amin (787–813) and al-Ma'mun (786–833). After his
death a civil war *(fitna)* broke out between al-Amin and al-Ma'mun. These
verses and others below are a few of the many poems written about that war.

She, with the eyes of a gazelle,
her teeth, a flash of lightning.

Other women, confused like virgins,
on their necks nice ornamental chains.

O brother! they cried, but there was no longer any brother,
he had already lost any sense of brotherhood.

People were removed from this world's shadow,
their belongings sold in markets.

And near the house a stranger was thrown
beheaded in the middle of the road.

Lying between rival camps,
nobody knew to whom he belonged.

No child cared for his father;
friends abandoned their friends.

Whatever I forget from my past experiences,
I will remember the house of the beloved.

Anon.

[*Compulsory Pilgrimage*]

They made their way to Mecca even if they did not intend
    to;[12]
they wanted to find refuge to escape al-Hirsh's violence.

Many a people were indeed content until
al-Hirsh was empowered to inflict punishment on them.

---

12. Written about the civil war between Harun ar-Rashid's sons al-Amin
and al-Ma'mun. Al-Hirsh was one of the active military commanders during
the war.

Mansur al-Namari (?–809)

[*Breeze*]

Tree branches in Baghdad, what a wonderful smell,
scores of lovely spots, to delight world and religion.

Breeze reviving the sick,
blowing between sweet basil branches.

Ashja' al-Sulami (?–810)

[*Palaces*]

Al-Salihiyya's[13] palaces — virgins
donning their garments for a wedding.

They overlook a valley, water's hands
covered the land with a garment weaved from flowers.

If the drizzle affects the earth,
the blossoms breathe without a breath.

The sky smeared the land with saffron,
in the morning their faces exciting men's desire.

---

13. One of Baghdad's neighborhoods.

Abu Nuwas (al-Hasan ibn Hani al-Hakami)
(747–62–813–15)

[Pilgrimage]

People say, Do you want to make the pilgrimage? Of course,
I say, only after Baghdad's delights expire.

Those of Qatrabbul included, and
Qubbat al-Firk, district of Kalwadha.

Al-Salihiyya too, also al-Karkh where
Baghdad's strangers gather — for me they are not strangers.[14]

How can I leave for Mecca, being still deeply engrossed
in a madam's brothel or in a tavern?

Let us say you save me from the pleasures of Baghdad, but
how can I free myself from Tayznabadh?[15]

---

14. In Arabic, *shudhdhadh Baghdad* — people who live in Baghdad but do
not belong to the city.

15. With the exception of Mecca, all places mentioned were in Baghdad and
its surrounds. These places were known for their taverns.

[Ships]

God made mounted beasts submissive to al-Amin.
He had never made them obedient even for kings.[16]

While the king's mounted beasts stride on the ground,
al-Amin passes on water, riding a forest lion.

A lion spreading his arms speeding,
the mouth wide, the teeth protruding.

He neither reins it in nor whips it;
thus does the Tigris when it flows over ships.

People wonder; they see in you a lion figure
progressing like passing clouds.

They praise God when they see you moving on it;
just imagine if they saw you on an eagle?[17]

With a hump and a beak and wings,
again and again cutting the waves.

Outstripping birds in the sky, if they
nudge it to move to and fro.

---

16. In Arabic, "the owner of the *mihrab*." The common meaning of *mihrab* is that semicircular niche in the wall of a mosque that indicates the *qibla*, the direction of the Kaaba in Mecca. In the early centuries of Islam, *mihrab* also meant the prestigious place for a king or any nobleman in a palace or house.
17. A ship in the shape of an eagle.

May God bless al-Amin and protect him;
may He preserve for him the fiber of youth.

He is a king panegyric poems can never suffice to describe;
Hashimi,[18] God made him to progress on the straight
    road.

[*April Morning*]

On an April morning, please drink with roses
from Qatrabbul's wine,[19] red as a rose.

Unrestrained, don't bother about any piety,
while you stay in Baghdad.

Soften your youthfulness with aged wine;
don't drink white honey like the inexperienced.

Befriend only those whose love for you in this world
    is pure.
Don't befriend those who cut the rope of love.

They refrain from you if you are poor,
befriending you only if you are rich.

---

18. Banu Hashim was a clan of the Quraysh tribe, of which Prophet
Muhammad was a member. His great-grandfather was Hashim, for whom
the clan is named.

19. Qatrabbul was a village near Baghdad that was known for its excellent
nabidh, an intoxicating drink made from different kinds of dates, or dates
mixed with raisins and honey.

'Inan (eighth century)

[Plowing][20]

Isn't it fair that he who knows
how to be angry, be forgiving?

Isn't it honorable for whom I have become
on earth a tillage to be plowed,[21] be satisfied?

---

20. 'Inan, Abu Nuwas's slave girl, fell in love with him; she sent him a
handkerchief with these verses.

21. Based on the Qur'an: "Your women are a tillage for you; so come unto
your tillage as you wish" (al-Baqara [The Cow], 223; translation according to
Arberry 1979 [1964]), p. 31).

'Amr ibn 'Abd al-Malik al-Warraq (?–815)

[An Evil Eye][22]

Oh Baghdad, who afflicted you with an evil eye?
Were not you the eye's delight?

Did not honorable people among your dwellers
engage with me in good deeds and favors?

Are not among your residents people whose
closeness was a symbol of glory?

Time wept over them like a crow of separation;
they perished, how hard the sorrow of separation hit me.

I uplift people to God whenever I mention them;
tears descend from my eye.

They were here, but Time dispersed and scattered them,
and Time is known to separate people.

How often they gladdened me in the face of Time's
    calamities;
how frequently they have helped me.

---

22. This poem and the next one were written about the civil war between
al-Amin and al-Ma'mun.

To God be attributed Time that assembled us.
Where have those days gone?

Oh you who destroyed Baghdad in order to dwell there,
you have destroyed yourselves in between those very two
     deeds.

The hearts of all people were one;
indeed, this was not only religion.

Taking them as prisoner you dispersed them;
all people are divided between two hearts.

[*Disgrace*]

Every day we have a breach we do not repair;
more and more they demand, less and less we have left.

When they destroy a house, we take the roofs,
and wait for the next.

They have narrowed every wide land in our country;
they now have wives here who will stay for good.

They use drums to summon in the prey; if they see
close up the face of the prey, they capture it.

They have corrupted the east of the country, the west
as well; we do not know which way to look.

When they come, they tell what they know;
if they see nothing, they forge ugly lies.

Noblemen are killed by a mere incitement,
a messenger of death spying all night.

Tahir ibn al-Husayn al-Khuza'i (776–822)

[*Your Night, Oh Baghdad*]

People say: Your night, Oh Baghdad,
is lovely, the air cool and fresh.

By my life, your night is thus only
because the day is beset by hellish wind.

A slight comfort after great agony,
and people say at once: What a paradise!

‘Ali ibn Jabala al-Ansari (known as al-‘Akawwak)
(776–828)

[*Exile*]

Truly, I grieve for Baghdad, what a town!
Midst my maladies, she has protected me.

Separating from her, I was Adam
expelled from Eden.

Ishaq al-Khuraymi (?–829)

[Elegy][23]

They said: Time never afflicted Baghdad;
she has not been wrecked by misfortunes.

She is like a bride, her barren places render
a young man full of respect, all the more so the fertile
    ones.

A paradise on earth, a prosperous abode,
calamities never frighten her.

The world yields her residents the abundance of her good
    things;
her misfortunes and difficulties become scanty.

She was opened to good things; her
population enjoyed her pleasures.

A dynasty of kings settled there,
mosques' pulpits were happy with them.

But Time has vicissitudes;
evil-doers continued to nibble at her kingdom.

---

23. Written after the civil war between al-Amin and al-Ma'mun.

Till she was steeped in a cup of
trial, whose offenses cannot be abolished.

After long companionship, the city split into groups,
the connections between them cut off.

Have you seen what kings have done
if they were not prevented by a good adviser?

Our kings brought themselves to an
abyss of wrongfulness, it is impossible to depart from.

What harm if they were faithful to the convent
and fortified their minds with fear of God;

Not shedding blood of their groups,
not obeying agitating youth?

Have you seen the flowering gardens,
the eyes of the educated always enjoy them?

Have you seen the palaces, their doors opening onto the
    streets,
their chambers concealing beautiful women?

Have you seen the villages where the
kings planted their green plains?

Surrounded by vineyards, palm trees, and basil;
now the sockets of their eyes are bleeding.

Vacant land, empty, dogs bark there;
the sand denies the existence of any traces of houses.

Now poverty never abandons her;
it has become her companion; gladness left her.

What a misfortune! Oh Baghdad, a kingdom with
calamities afflicting her residents.

God has granted her His grace, but when her deadly sins
enveloped her, He punished her.

With drowning, stoning, burning, and war
that started to dog her existence.

Religion there has weakened, noblemen
despised, the immoral surpassing in generosity the pious.

The slave has shattered the pride of his master
and enslaved noblewomen.

Among the protégés, the noble have become the most
      evil.
He who had been afraid of roads has become the master.

Have you seen the woman bereft of her child, yelling
on the road? The effort has overcome her; she runs

After a bier on which lies her only son,
stabbed in his breast.

Hopefully time could change either for the
good or slip into scary blunders — I wish I knew.

Will our earth revert to what it was,
now that our circumstances brought us to this pass?

Ishaq al-Mawsili (767–850)

[*Weeping*]

Do you weep over Baghdad though she is still close?
What will happen tomorrow when you are far away?

By your life, I did not leave Baghdad willingly,
I would have stayed had I any choice.

When my soul remembers Baghdad, it
is shattered from longing, nearly perishing from desire.

Suffice that I am sad because I could not
bid her farewell, nor have any relationship with any of her
    dwellers.

Al-Husayn ibn al-Dahhak (778–870)

[*Only Sorrow*][24]

Among the violations of your[25] sanctity they abused,
behind curtains, the Prophet's female descendants' honor.

Your relatives remained in their places and failed to help.
All of them admitted humiliation.

Their virgin females showed their ankles
in grief, as they wept their demand for justice.

Garments were stolen, veiled women
were exposed, earrings were removed.

While being assaulted they seemed as
pearls emerging from oysters.

You are a king whose kingdom has been betrayed by Fate;
these are misfortunes of Time.

After you, how could we retain
any semblance of glory? How could any honor still be
    ours?

---

24. Watching the women in the Caliph's palace during the civil war
between al-Amin and al-Ma'mun, al-Husayn ibn al-Dahhak composed these
verses.
25. al-Amin.

Oh man whose slumber is betrayed by sleeplessness,
sorrows appeared and your heart is grieving.

You were the only hope I relied on;
now there is only sorrow.

Affairs are disturbed; evil is reckoned
usual; goodness is denied.

Because you are absent, the union has fragmented,
the world is neglected, the heart has become dark.

[Their Veils Were Torn][26]

What made my heart sorrowful and my tears flow is
the violation of the Prophet's female descendants' honor.

In al-Khuld their veils were torn,
young women with raised breasts exposed like rays of sun.

One woman, feeling shy after removing her robe,
was humbled and started weeping.

A herd of gazelles from the highest nobles of Banu
    Hashim
claimed relationship to the best of the living and the dead.

Whenever I recall them, my hand is repelled
from the fire of my warm liver and broken heart.

God, may the night of the malicious be without joy;
may their hopes never come true.

---

26. The poet was a supporter of al-Amin in his struggle with his brother
al-Ma'mun. In these verses, he describes the slave girls of al-Khuld Palace
(Palace of Paradise) in Baghdad and how they were exposed to humiliation,
abuse, and rape.

'Abd Allah ibn Tahir (798–844)

[The Wailing Pigeon][27]

A pigeon, a ring on her neck, wailed in Bab al-Taq;
my abundant tears flowed down.

She used to sing on trees; maybe
she sang on trunk's branches.

Separation hurled her into Iraq; now
instead of in trees she moans in markets.

She lost her offspring; her tears fell incessantly —
tears reveal the soul yearning.

May separation be destroyed; may the vein of its heart be
    cut!
May a barman water it with a black serpent's poison!

What did it intend by sending a pigeon
with never an inkling of what Baghdad had become
    among the lands?

---

27. In Bab al-Taq, one of the neighborhoods of Baghdad, there used to be a
bird market. It was said that anyone who had a problem should buy a bird
and free it; then his or her troubles would end. 'Abd Allah ibn Tahir stayed in
Baghdad and the Caliph refused to meet him. Once he was passing near the
bird market and heard a pigeon wailing. He wanted to buy and free it, but the
owner refused to sell it for less than 500 dirhams. Finally, he bought and
freed it and composed these verses.

The same misfortune, Oh pigeon, has stricken me.
    Please beg
the One who loosed your chains also to loose mine!

[Dung][28]

Oh Baghdad, when it rains or wind strikes,
you are nothing but dung;
when you are dry, you are only evil dust.

---

28. This poetic text is rare in that it consists of three hemistichs.

[Tranquil Abode]

Have you seen in any corner of the world
a tranquil abode like Baghdad?!

Here, life is pure, green, and fresh;
in other places life is neither gentle nor cool.

Life here is longer, the food is wholesome;
indeed, parts of the earth are better than others.

God commanded that no caliph will pass away
there; He decrees whatever He desires.[29]

A stranger can sleep here; unlike Damascus
where a stranger cannot close his eyes.

When Baghdad is compensated favorably,
it is because she preceded in giving good.

When she is destined to be hated and deserted,
she does not deserve hatred and desertion.

---

29. According to the court astrologer Abu Sahl ibn Nawbakht (d. 786),
before building Baghdad, al-Mansur asked him to look in the stars and his
verdict was unambiguous: no caliph will pass away there. Indeed most
caliphs passed away while away from Baghdad.

[Nothing Is Like Baghdad]

There is nothing like Baghdad, worldly-wise and
    religious,
despite Time's transitions.

Between Qatrabbul and Karkh, a narcissus
blooms; so do a gillyflower garden and wild roses.

May God bless these high palaces, and the
gazelles with beautiful eyes who dwell there.

Souls thrive on the sweet fragrance emanating from her,
protected among basil leaves.

The Tigris flows among them; you can see
black ships rising like mules.

Houses overlook courtyards with open doors,
made beautiful with decorations and ornaments.

Palaces are there, with wings that fly
visitors to the people who are hosts.

From every ship's spine emerges a palace,
made of precious teak tree with columns of stones.

'Ali ibn al-Jahm (804–63)

[Does' Eyes]

Does' eyes between al-Rusafa[30] and the bridge
carried desire from places I know or know not.

They revived inside me old longing — there has been no
solace — adding burning coals to those already afire.

They were safe, leaving hearts
to be pierced by brown spears' blades.

We are moons, they said,
only lighting a road at night, not welcoming everyone.

There is no offering but what the onlooker is provided
    with;
there is no union but for the journeying imagination.

They dislodged the heart from its place,
inflaming what is between breast and ribs.

I wish they had targeted me with great despair
or betrayed me before I attained old age.

Alas, youthfulness is now far behind — does should
be hunted only when you are young and rich.

---

30. Al-Rusafa is a quarter on the eastern shore of the Tigris in Baghdad.

Old age scares them — we sometimes see them squeeze
fingers between breasts and neck.

We spent the night despite slanderers,
as if we were a mixture of rain and wine.

If they ignore or deny a promise they give,
it is nothing new or strange for beautiful girls.

Oh my dear friends, sweet is love, bitter as well;
love has let me taste both, sweetness and bitterness.

No more dealing with love and pushing away old age;
I wish love could be dispelled by scolding.

By what is forbidden between us, have you ever seen
anything more tender than complaint, more cruel than
    separation?

Or anything more eloquent than a lover's eye in exposing
    his secret,
for sure when it lets a teardrop fall?

I will never forget how she said to her companion:
Look what desire has done to that nobleman.

Why does he suffer so? asked her companion.
Do you have an excuse for killing?

Were he to meet you, love might revive him. Did you
not realize that the prisoner of love is in the most cruel of jails?

I drive people away from him, she said, rarely is love
sweet for her whose veil is not torn.

They were aware I overheard them and said:
Who listens in secret without our knowledge?

A man who can conceal his desire if you wish, I said,
otherwise, he will not restrain himself and give free rein.

But he complains she is mean and miserly,
neither smiling nor rejoicing.

We have been scolded, she said. Correct, I replied.
Evil should only be removed by evil.

As if I am disreputable through verses, she said,
speaking about us in one city, then in another.

You think badly of me, I said. I am not a poet even if
my heart is sometimes filled with poetry.

Not everyone riding a horse can control it;
not everyone who makes a horse run is an equestrian.

Please ask whoever you want — he will tell you:
I am for always an excellent keeper of secrets.

I am not a man whose name is circulated by poets;
it is my fame that makes my poetry well known.

Poetry has many followers — I have never followed its path,
neither in hardship nor in prosperity.

Poetry is not a shade in which you find refuge;
it has never raised my worth nor hurt my merit.

[*At al-Karkh's Gate*]

We stepped into al-Karkh's Gate, the best of all houses,
opposite us, the beautiful slave girls of al-Mufaddal.

Ibn Surayj, al-Gharid, and Ma'bad[31] have
valuable songs for our ears — there are no substitutes.

Cheerful young women, not bashful with guests;
their master is neither frightening nor arrogant.

He is happy when a guest has no shyness;
he turns a blind eye, though he is mindful.

In his house, use your hands, carefree.
Do not be afraid of the master; do whatever you want.

Hint with your hand, wink, do not fear
any watcher if you are not niggardly.

Keep a distance from the lamp — curse it;
as soon as the lamp is extinguished, approach and kiss.

---

31. Three of the most famous male singers from the early Islamic period.

Ask! — nothing is forbidden — say whatever you want;
sleep with no fear; get up without any hurry.

The house is yours, as long as your presents are generous,
as long as you sip the honeyed drink.

Exploit the days of your youth; all of them will pass
and perish, disappointment will soon be revealed.

Life is only a night whose end projects
us into a day of hastened pleasure.

May God bless al-Karkh's Gate, a wonderful place of
     pleasures,
including al-Waddah Palace[32] and Birkat Zalzal.[33]

[*Ceaseless Rain*]

When rain noticed the good moist earth contracted into
     lumps,
because of its failure, with the hills wanting more;

And when rain saw the regions of Iraq in need
of water, it went on raining copiously.

The rain did not leave Baghdad until it flooded
valleys that could not contain the influx.

---

32. The palace of the Caliph al-Mahdi (reigned 775–85) near al-Rusafa.
33. Bordering al-Karkh's Gate was an artificial pond, Birkat Zalzal.

Until we could see birds flying so low in her quarters,
beautiful girls were able to catch them in their hands.

Until Baghdad was covered with blossoms,
as if she were a bride, her striped garment making her
    behave proudly.

Until the Tigris became like a double coat of mail,
with rings, the iron of which alternately emerges and
    disappears.

Until the rain had given Iraq and its people their full due,
only then did a messenger come from the north wind.[34]

---

34. In the region of Baghdad, the north wind signals dryness and the end of
rains.

'Abd Allah ibn Muhammad al-Bafi (?–893)

[*Communion*]

Peace be upon Baghdad, a mine of every good,
an abode delighting all onlookers.

Peace be upon her whenever the eyes
of the beloved wound those of lovers.

Unwillingly we came to her, but once
we got used to her, we were unwilling to depart.

We have no longing for places, but
the bitterest of life is separation from your beloved.

Ibn Dust (ninth century)

[Tuesday]

Each night, the moon disappears but returns;
so why have you disappeared from my eyes for three
    nights?

If you do not come on Monday evening,
Tuesday you will not find me.

**Abu Muhammad al-Hasan ibn
Ahmad al-Brujardi (ninth century)**

[*Tuesday Is for Pleasure*]

Tuesday is for pleasure —
it is forbidden to ignore.

Fate is blind; your life
will not be pleasant.

Thus, *carpe diem,* hurry and enjoy;
the rule, by God, is for an impetuous person.

al-Walid ibn 'Ubayd Allah al-Buhturi (820–97)

[*Desire between Ribs*]

Desire mutters between ribs;
heart's memory always whispers.

A man may be spared his anguish when
traveling on gloomy nights upon a young, running she-camel.

Baghdad dealt wrongly with me; she was cruel
to her visitor though she is the most friendly abode.

I have neither gain nor companionship from my tribe;
nor does Persia express any friendship.

Please tell the prince, only he is the moon;
Time smiles for him, even while frowning.

You have favored people lagging behind me and failing;
they humiliated me; enviers and rivals rejoice.

In the train of verses, I alone excel — no contenders;
famous in the East, in the West as well, anywhere.

I send the most beautiful of these verses
as brides for you.

Farewell, I am leaving!
My verses, a gift to your glory.

Ibn al-Rumi (836–96)

[*Tuesday Is Not Only Tuesday*][35]

Tuesday? What is Tuesday?
It is raised high in the pick of the days.

A center in the middle of the week,
a pearl necklace decorating a beautiful woman.

God would not have let *Nayruz* be on Tuesday,
if it had not gathered together all joys.

[*Imagination*]

A city where I accompanied childhood and youthfulness;
there I wore a new cloak of glory.

When she appears in the imagination, I see on her
budding branches aflutter.

---

35. This poem is about a coincidence when the Feast of *Nayruz* happened to
be on Tuesday.

[*Wahid, the Singer*]

Oh my friends, Wahid's[36] love has enslaved me;
my heart is sick, I suffer.

A tree-branch has lent her a slender stature;
from the gazelle she has borrowed eyes and neck.

Her hair and cheeks shine
in blackness and redness.

Charm ignites its own fire because of Wahid,
on a cheek with no wrinkles.

With the cheeks she is coolness and peace;[37]
for lovers she is great distress.

Whatever water is warmed by her cheeks,
sucking her saliva is coolness.

Her honor has been never damaged;
she has melted lovers' hearts even if they are iron.

Water that her cheeks has boiled
cannot be cooled but by sipping her saliva.

---

36. A singer who rose to fame in Baghdad due to her brilliant voice and
exquisite beauty.

37. Based on the Qur'an: "We said: 'O fire, be coolness and safety for
Abraham!'" (*al-Anbiya'* [The Prophets] 69; translation according to Arberry
1979 [1964], p. 328).

That very saliva could have quenched my desire,
if only she had not refused to let me drink more.

One inexperienced requested her description.
Two matters, I said, easy and hard:

It is easy to say she is the best among
all, but it is hard to be specific.

Sun with abundant rain, both luminaries, the sun
and full moon, benefit from her light.

When she appears to onlookers, her beauty
causes some to feel poor and others happy.

A gazelle dwelling in hearts, healing them,
a dove with its beautiful song.

She sings spontaneously and effortlessly;
brilliant in singing, her limbs are calm.

Her brows never furrow with effort,
her veins never swell.

In silence without interruption;
her voice vibrantly flowing.

Her voice projected far by her breath,
a long breath like her lovers' sighs.

Her coyness and amorous gestures soften the voice;
the sorrow thins it out, till it nearly dies.

At times the voice dies; at others it is full of life;
both simple and complex singing — pure pleasure.

Her voice has molded decorations and ornaments from
melody — the melody is proud.

May her mouth be sweet; to what she repeats,
everything can bear witness.

Accumulated water can remove thirst; singing
can revive lost happiness.

Whoever kisses her asks for more;
whoever listens to her wishes more.

For love of her kind, the most restrained person
turns lively, brisk; the believer deviates from the straight
        way.

She never communicates with hearts, but inflicts them
with her love as she wishes.

The string she plays with —
a bow string that looses an arrow at war.

When she draws the string for drinkers,
they are sure she will hit.

Singing, she is like Maʿbad and Ibn Surayj,
playing strings, like Zalzal and ʿAqid.[38]

Her only fault: when she sings for noblemen,
they become enslaved by her.

She tempts their hearts to love her even more,
but they had no more to offer.

[Red-Dyed Finger]

She stood determinedly at Bab al-Taq,
a gazelle from the well-guarded women of Iraq.

She is seven plus four plus three of age;
she has imprisoned her longing lover's heart.

Who are you, Oh gazelle? I asked. I am, she responded,
from the gentle art of the Creator.

Do not try to touch us! she warned: look at this finger,
we dipped it into lovers' blood.

---

38. Maʿbad and Ibn Surayj — famous singers; Zalzal and ʿAqid — famous
slave-girl musicians.

Adam ibn 'Abd al-'Aziz al-Umawi (ninth century)

[Deprived of Sleep]

My night in Baghdad became longer; whoever spends a
    night in
Baghdad will stay awake, deprived of sleep.

As soon as day escapes, it becomes a land where
    mosquitoes
swarm, in pairs and alone.

Humming, their bellies white as if they were
pack mules repelled by spears.

Abu al-'Aliya (ninth century)

[The Hand of Generosity Is Crippled]

Leave! Baghdad is not a place to stay in.
There is no benefit from her.

She is a place for kings, their wickedness seen in their
    faces,
all of them devoid of any glory.

Except those who are generous, their number so scarce,
they are given only to Baghdad.

No wonder, the hand of generosity is crippled.
Charity from benefactors has become rare.

When the waves of the abundant sea boil,
all rivers most certainly overflow.

'Ali ibn Abi Hashim (tenth century)

[*Builders Build for Ruins*]

They build and say: We shall never die, but
builders build for ruins.

I have never encountered an intelligent person
untroubled by the anticipated ruination.

'Abd Allah ibn al-Mu'tazz (861–909)

[*The Traces of Her Bite*]

Oh night of mine at al-Karkh, please persist;
Oh night, don't go, please don't go.

A messenger came with news of a visit,
after long separation and anger.

An apple in his palm, the traces
of her bite — a scorpion's claws.

[*Squeezed by an Old Woman*]

In Baghdad, night made my sorrow deepen.
If you leave her, you may win or lose.

Unwillingly, I stayed there, as if I were an
impotent man being squeezed by an old woman.

[*Thick Smoke*]

How can I sleep while I am in
Baghdad? Living there, never leaving her.

A land over whose wells
hover crowns of mosquitoes.

Winter and summer, the air is
thick smoke, the water dirty.

Oh king's abode, you used
to spread musk when a breeze was blowing.

How did she become deserted? Time has defeated her,
the owl of bad luck is the only source of life.

We used to be her true residents, but that
time has gone; nothing is everlasting.

[*Waistbands*]

In Baghdad, I got lessons in weaving waistbands.
Before imprisonment, I had been a king.

After riding noble horses, I was chained.
This is because of changing constellations.

[*White Roses*]

To whoever reproaches me today for drunkenness, I have
    no excuse;
give me the big cup, give the others the small one.

Alienated from the clouds, the sun
disappeared; you could not see any sign of it.

The burden was too heavy for the clouds; there was no
earth in Baghdad except being in need of rain.

The clouds' eyes were bathed in water.
All at once they poured down snow, spreading it like white
  roses.

[*Full of Blood*]

Suffering at night, my eyelids still open;
sparks of fire sting my skin.

Birds blow in the ears,
full of blood, brimming.

Muhammad ibn Dawud al-Isfahani (868–909)

[*Pain of Skinning*]

My heart is in love with al-Karkh, ardent love;
it is the love solely of one who has lived there.

After I lost her, death became the refuge;
the slaughtered are never troubled by the pain of skinning.

'Ubayd Allah ibn 'Abd Allah ibn Tahir (?–913)

[*Could a Lover Leave?*]³⁹

Could a lover leave, while the beloved is left behind?
Could love's ardor survive, while pleasure vanishes?

I salute you, Oh Baghdad, house of pleasures
as long as my eyes have light.

I never left her out of hate;
Time targeted me with its violent blow.

Is there no protector? No refuge?
No shelter from this calamity?

I wish our happy time together would return;
the lover would come back, the beloved would rejoice.

---

39. 'Ubayd Allah ibn 'Abd Allah ibn Tahir was appointed governor of
Yemen. He was sad to leave Baghdad and composed these verses.

ʿAli ibn al-Husayn al-Wasiti (?–919)

[Temple for the Hearts]

Is there any equivalent to the City of Peace?!
A miracle! You will not find for Baghdad any parallel.

A temple for the hearts, spring
there everlasting, even in summer.

A city for all noble traits, where
the meaning of everything shines like the sun.

al-Husayn ibn Mansur al-Hallaj (858–922)

[Tell the Gazelle]

Oh breeze, please tell the gazelle
water only increases thirst.

I have a lover; His love is ever inside me;
if He wishes to walk, He can do it on my cheeks.

His soul is mine — mine His;
if He wishes, I too wish; if I wish, He does too.

[Ordained by Christ]

Please tell the beloved, I sailed out to sea;
the ship broke apart; my death is ordained by Christ.

I have no need for places, neither wide nor narrow.
I do not need any cities.

[I Am Whom I Love]

I am whom I love, whom I love is me;
two souls occupying one body.

Since we fell in love, people see us as one;
if you see me, you see Him.

His soul, mine; mine, His;
who has ever seen twin souls in one body?

[*States*]

Silence, quietness, and mutism.
Knowledge, ecstasy, and grave.

Mud, fire, and light.
Cold, shadow, and sun.

Mountain, plain, and desert.
River, sea, and wasteland.

Intoxication, sobriety, and longing.
Proximity, unification, and intimacy.

Contraction, unfolding, and erasure.
Taking, giving, and attracting.

Describing, exposing, and dressing.
This is people's language.

In their eyes, the world equals ten cents,
mere noises behind a door when you are close to Him.

Your language, mere whispering;
a believer never aspires to assets and pleasures.

He is a servant of illusions
but the Truth is glorified and holy.

Abu 'Abd Allah Ibrahim ibn
Muhammad Niftawayhi (858–935)

[Perpetual Rain]

Clouds water al-Karkh with perpetual rain,
unceasingly falling, never stopping.

These abodes possess beauty and joy.
They have advantages over any other abode.

Anon. (tenth century)

[*Only Death*][40]

After I had stripped her of her clothes, she said,
Aren't you afraid of your relatives or mine?

We are each afraid from within our own placement, I
    replied,
but isn't it only a matter of your death or mine?

---

40. These verses are found written on the chair of one of the court jesters in Baghdad.

Anon. (tenth century)

[*The Breast Beater*]

This minister — a minister in stupidity,
no sooner appointing than dismissing.

In his office, he assembles bribers and campaigners;
the best merchandiser is the winner.

I beseech you not to reproach him;
he barely escaped beggary.

Ibn al-Tammar al-Wasiti (tenth century)

[*Golden Bridge*]

Rise, resist misfortunes and catastrophes,
gather in your cup pleasures and amusements.

Don't you see the armies of night escaping,
defeated, while the armies of morning are waiting?

Full moon sits on the western horizon as though
a golden bridge stretching between the two banks.

'Ali ibn Muhammad al-Tanukhi (892–953)

[Moon and River]

What a beautiful river when night falls!
The moon stirs westward toward the horizon;

The Tigris on the moon, a blue carpet;
the moon over the river, a golden veil.

Mansur ibn Kayaghlagh (?–960)

[*Moon*]

Time has restored my beloved, you may reproach me;
my friends, please let me drink, and drink yourselves.

Many a night did I spend with her full moon
hovering over the Tigris before it disappeared.

The cupbearer passed around the wine;
I imagined he was a full moon bearing a star.

When the moon is about to set, it is
a golden sword unsheathed over the water.

Abu Ishaq al-Sabi (925–94)

[Basra and Baghdad]

Alas, I deeply miss Baghdad;
I miss her snowy water.

Here, in ugly Basra, we are watered
with only sickly, yellowish drinks.

How could we be satisfied drinking it, while in our own
    land,
we clean our asses with purer water?!

Abu al-Hasan 'Ali ibn 'Abd al-'Aziz al-Jurjani
(928–1002)

[*Garments of Mourning*]

Will those nights bring back a reunion,
or should I not wait for that any longer?

Will I again befriend my beloved? Since we parted, I wear
only garments of mourning, never changing to others.

When only a glimpse of light emerges from Baghdad,
my bed repels my body, sleep escapes me.

If morning clouds do not keep their promises of
watering Baghdad, my tears will do that.

I wish for all clouds to water Baghdad's banks,
like tears of a lover.

She is the home of elegant women, their eyes,
gazelle-like, offer no escape for the lover.

There dwells the irrepressible soul
that is never satisfied without the beloved heart.

Every heart longs for her, as if her
very quarters were built from hearts.

All her nights are full of youthful love;
all her seasons are spring.

[*Downpour of Tears*]

I wish Baghdad's quarters to be watered by an abundance
    of rain,
just like the downpour of my tears.

I left there a heart, its longing saddens me;
I left there a soul I cannot forget.

I would forgive Time for all its calamities
if only I could visit her after the long separation.

al-Sharif al-Radi (930–77)

[Camels' Saliva]

I see Baghdad, hit by snow,
attacking early in the morning.

As if the tips of her landmarks were burdened she-camels
with their skins removed.

As if the snow were camels' saliva poured
like a torrent, shot from a waterwheel.

It covered uplands, every valley;
upon its elevated spots a new white veil.

All valleys were smitten by snow;
all plains and uplands became dust colored.

Wherever you look from the hills,
you see only white; the consequence is only dark.

I say to the snow, as it hits
lands, more strongly or less:

Beware! Human minds are ice for any
generosity, favors are chilly.

If you want to pile up more miseries on the ones already
existing, you will never succeed.

al-Tahir ibn al-Muzaffar ibn Tahir al-Khazin
(tenth century?)

[Sweeter than Wine]

May God water with morning rain, the place in
Baghdad, between al-Khuld, al-Karkh, and the bridge.

This is a beautiful city that grants her residents
things never conjoined elsewhere since they were created.

Tender weather, balanced and healthy,
the water — what a taste! Sweeter than wine!

Her Tigris, two banks arrayed for us like pearls in a
    necklace,
a crown beside a crown, a palace beside a palace.

Her soil, musk; her water, silver;
her gravel, diamonds and jewels.

'Ali ibn al-Faraj al-Shafi'i (tenth century?)

[Elephants on Mercury]

How wonderful is the bridge, stretching over the Tigris,
great in perfection, saturated with glamor and beauty.

Glory and honor to Iraq, consolation
and solace for gloomy lovers.

Curiously, when approaching and fixing your eyes on it,
you see a perfumed line written on parchment.

Or an ivory with ebony decorations —
elephants stepping on soil of mercury.

Muhammad ibn 'Abd Allah al-Salami (947–1002)

[Busy Square]

I see a busy square, galloping horses
leading armored fighters. Nobody leads them.

Once I was riding for pleasure on a noble horse,
with a body but no heart.

Galloping on, I imagined the ground was a woman's face;
the Tigris was her eye; the horse, her darting gaze.

Ma'dan al-Taghlibi (eleventh century)

[Promised Land]

Baghdad, a true abode, its perfume captivating,
its breeze reviving people's hearts.

Suitable for the rich, not for common people
who sleep in poverty and need.

Had Korah, the god of opulence, resided there,
he would have become anxious and frightened.

She is like a promised land, but
hastening to provide food and garments.

Women with beautiful eyes and soft young men,
all pleasures you desire are here, but not gentle people.

Abu Saʻd Muhmmad ibn ʻAli ibn Khalaf al-Nayramani (?–1023)

[I Am Your Ransom]

Oh friends of mine in Baghdad, are you
still faithful or has our friendship worn out?

On the day of farewell, did your eyes shed tears
for me? Mine still weeping, morning and evening.

When you talk of distant friends,
do you speak well of me?

Oh Baghdad, I wish all cities to be your ransom,
even my path, even my abode.

I have wandered through lands, East and West;
I led my horses there, the camels as well.

Never have I seen such a homeland as Baghdad;
never have I seen a river such as the Tigris;

Nor such residents — tender qualities,
sweet speeches, good thoughts, and ideas.

People challenge me: If your love for Baghdad was genuine, why did you leave? I give them my answer:

The rich remain in their land,
while the poor are tossed away by Fate.

'Ali ibn Zurayq Abu al-Hasan al-Baghdadi (?–1029)

[Moon over Baghdad]

Please do not reproach him;[41] it could pain him;
you are right, but he does not listen.

With your reproaches, you crossed the limit,
though your only intention was for the good.

Please be tender while scolding;
his heart is exhausted; it aches.

Suffice the anguish of separation,
relentlessly he is tortured by discord.

When he returns from a journey,
another troubles him; there is never a meeting.

Always he camps and travels, as if he were
entitled to stroll through lands.

In Baghdad, God reserved for me a moon;[42]
in al-Karkh, it rises from the orbit of buttons.

---

41. The masculine beloved in Arabic love poems may refer to both male and
female.

42. The poet had to leave behind his beloved named Qamar (in Arabic,
moon). Here, it makes sense to write Qamar "it," because the poet evokes an
image of the moon.

I bade him farewell, but I wish the luxury of living
had bid me farewell instead.

How much he wanted me to linger till noon;
but exigencies could not be avoided.

How strongly did he grasp me on the day of farewell;
my tears were flowing, his as well.

I cannot lie; separation has ripped the cloth of
my patience; I patch it up.

I try to pardon him for the crime of
abandoning me, but for that there is no forgiveness.

Since I left his bed,
sleep has escaped my eyes.

So many days I have wasted in sorrow; I wish
the nights that exhausted our bodies to unite us again.

I had never thought Fate would afflict me with
such love or his as well.

I was always afraid of parting, without preparing a
     shield;
so many days I have wasted in sorrow.

If death attacks one of us,
what can he do in the face of God's destiny?

[*Baghdad's People*]

I have traveled far to find a parallel for Baghdad
and her people — my task was second to despair.

Alas, for me Baghdad is the entire world,
her people — the only genuine ones.

Abu Muhammad 'Abd al-Wahhab al-Maliki (?–1031)

[Baghdad's Air]

Baghdad's wonderful air increases my longing;
I wish I could be close to her despite impeding Fate.

How could I desert her today when she has united
the best of twins: love and air?[43]

[A Qur'an in an Unbeliever's House]

Baghdad is a fine home for the wealthy,
but an abode of misery and distress for the poor.

I walked among them in dismay
as though I were a Qur'an in an unbeliever's house.

---

43. In Arabic, the words are very similar: *hawa* — love; *hawa'* — air.

[*Like a Friend*][44]

Peace be upon Baghdad from wherever I stay,
she deserves my blessings twofold and more.

By God, I honestly swear I left her not for want of love,
I know well her two banks.

But her vastness for me became cramped,
daily bread unattainable.

She is like a friend to whom I want to be close,
but his traits push me away from him.

---

44. The poet decided to leave for Egypt and Baghdadi people turned out to
bid him farewell, expressing regret about his departure. He replied: "If I
could find any quantity of broad beans every day, I would never leave."
During his journey to Egypt he composed these verses.

al-Sharif al-Murtada (965–1044)

[*Gazelle*]

Near al-Karkh, in Baghdad, we suddenly
saw a gazelle; people were shooing her away.

Her braids, sword-belts for her eyeball-knives;
The sword's scabbard, her eyelid; the blade, each eyelash.

Her two plaits conspired to kill me —
have you ever seen a poet assassinated by hair?

Abu al-'Ala' al-Ma'arri (973–1058)

[*Love*]

We fell in love with Iraq when we were young;
only being middle-aged were we lucky to meet her.

We approached the water of the Tigris, unparalleled;
we visited the noblest trees, the date palms.

We quenched our thirst, without ever gratifying our desire;
what a pity, nothing in this world will survive.

[*Farewell*]

Oh people of Baghdad, I bid you farewell; my heart
is full of sighs that never tire of stinging.

Damascus and her people are unworthy substitutes,
though my home is there and they are my own people.

Give me just one more drink;
if I could, I would sip all the waters of the Tigris.

[Sadness]

Oh my brothers, between the Euphrates and Jillaq,[45]
I will not inform you of impossibilities.

Please let it be known: I remember my commitments;
I never humiliated my face to beg.

I never visited Baghdad for glory and prices
as did Ghalyan when he visited Bilal.[46]

I was envied only because of my graciousness;
I have neither money nor supporters.

[Deserted Beloved]

In Baghdad, we have people we want to salute;
please do it on our behalf; may God salute you.

Two things make me sad: a mother whom
I have not seen for so long, and a diminishing wealth.

May God water the Tigris; Fate separates among people;
any constellation's reunion soon ends in separation.

---

45. Another name for Damascus.

46. The poet Dhu al-Ruma Ghaylan ibn 'Uqba (696–735) used to visit the
Emir Bilal ibn Abi Burda al-Ash'ari to praise him and get grants.

Unlike me, al-Walid[47] has condemned staying there:
"Baghdad dealt wrongly with me," he said. God forbid!

If I meet al-Walid, and the destination is the Day of
   Judgment,
I will not spare him my reproach.

[*Oh Treasurer!*]

My friends, I am not so young;
please free me, the chains so hurt me.

I need only one thing from Iraq and its people;
if you can provide it, compensation will be sure.

Please ask the scholars on both banks, ask as well the
   fellows
staying there for learning, until their hair becomes grey.

Do they have any advice to console a beggar?
His convoy cannot find the right way.

I want only to visit friends; they are true
people; I do not want a bride nor to enjoy the river.

Forcing me to leave was he that tempted Adam and Eve
from the sky to fall to the earth.[48]

---

47. The poet al-Walid ibn 'Ubayd Allah al-Buhturi.
48. Referring to Iblis, Satan in Arab tradition.

Oh treasurer of the House of Knowledge, so many
    deserts
separate us, full of voices of demons and partridges.

If horses of speech bolt, you
can control them with their reins.

Fright never caused me to neglect your friendship;
there we should observe only discipline.

Maybe Time will be satisfied and free me from my chains,
or perhaps it is always angry.

Abu al-Ma'ali (1028–85)

[Bearded Boy]

Look for another! they urged.
In that case I will never be pleased, I replied.

If his saliva were not honey,
the bees would never have invaded his mouth.

Abu al-Fadl ibn Muhammad al-Khazin al-Katib (?–1131)

['Antar and 'Abla]

I am scared of him when he is drunk; noticing my horror
he shows a dignified and sober face.

He is 'Antar; if you wish, he could be 'Ablah as well;[49]
a lion in war or a gazelle for copulation.

[No Nobleman in the Valley]

When God rains on the earth,
may He not rain on Baghdad.

The nobleman there is lost; as the proverb
says: "No nobleman in the valley."

There you can find all you want, pursuers of evil, whores,
pimps or clowns who for amusement slap you.

---

49. 'Antar — a hero of romances of chivalry; 'Abla — his sweetheart.

Usama ibn Munqidh (1095–1188)

[*Scales of Justice*]

They had described Baghdad for me,
but when I visited her, I saw the best of cities.

Beautiful venue, high-minded people,
they are charming and generous.

They have no defects, except they insist on not
cheating — from every finger dangle the scales of justice.

Muhammad ibn Ahmad ibn Shumay'a al-Baghdadi
(thirteenth century)

[*The "How Are You?" People*]

Friendship of al-Zawra's[50] residents is falsehood,[51]
residents' warmth as well — don't be tempted.

Baghdad is a place for a mere "How are you?"
You will not be able to gain more.

---

50. Al-Zawra' (The Bent or the Crooked) is one of the names of Baghdad.
One explanation is that the city took the name from the Tigris, which was
bent as it passed by the city.

51. In Arabic, *zur* (falsehood) from the same root as al-Zawra'.

Muhyi al-Din ibn al-'Arabi (1165–1240)[52]

[*Melancholic Dove*]

Oh you, the ben-tree[53] of the valley
on Baghdad river's bank.

A melancholic dove on a swaying bough
filled me with grief.

Its singing reminding me
of the chamber lady's tune.

Fine-tuning her triple cords,
do not mention al-Hadi's brother.[54]

Excelling in singing, the camel driver
Anjasha[55] — nothing beyond her.

---

52. The poet himself provided a mystical commentary on his own collection, *Tarjuman al-Ashwaq* (The Interpreter of Desires), from which the following poems have been taken. Most of the notes below rely on the commentary.

53. The ben-tree *(ban)* is the tree of light.

54. Al-Hadi, the fourth Abbasid caliph (reigned 785–86). His younger brother was Harun al-Rashid.

55. A camel driver from the time of the Prophet who used to sing so sweetly that the camels died.

I swear by Dhu al-Khadimat[56] where Salma[57] stays,
then on the right by Sindad.[58]

I'm in love with she who
dwells in Ajyad.[59]

No, I was mistaken,
she resides in the depths of my liver.

Confronted with her, beauty is confused.
Fragrance of musk and melodies scattered all around.

[The Most Beloved City]

The most beloved of the cities of God, after Medina,
Mecca, and Jerusalem, is Baghdad.

Can I not love the City of Peace, where
the righteous Imam of my faith and belief lives.

A Persian virgin stayed there as well,
soft, attractive to the eyes.

She revives whoever is slain by her eyes,
always offering beauty and generosity.

---

56. Probably Naqi' al-Khadimat near Madina.

57. A name for "the beloved," which poets used in their love poems.

58. A place on the western bank of the Euphrates.

59. A place at Mecca, but also, literally, necks. The poet interpreted it as referring to the places in the throat through which the breath passes.

Majd al-Din Husayn ibn al-Dawami
(thirteenth century)

[*Earthquake*]⁶⁰

While the leader of the true religion's army battalions
is visible, and the invasion has begun, I say:

If even the earth is shaken,
what would the enemy's soldiers' hearts feel?

---

60. On Sunday, March 13, 1244, while the Mongol forces were besieging
Baghdad, three earthquakes shook Baghdad. There were no injuries or
damage, but in the shadow of the Mongol threat, poets wrote about the event
as illustrating how the enemy feared the caliph's army.

al-Majd al-Nashabi (?–1259)

[*Turning a Child's Hair White*]

Heresy fanned a fire; Islam was burned,
no hope of the fire being quenched.

Oh grief, what a loss for the kingdom, for true religion,
what a loss — Baghdad struck with misery.

Death is touching me;
death is doing what it wants.

It is a dark cruel catastrophe
which turns a child's head and liver white.

Taqi al-Din ibn Abi al-Yusr (1193–1273)

[*Burned to Ashes*]

Oh seekers of news about Baghdad, the tears will tell you:
No benefit from remaining here, the beloved has departed.

Oh visitors to al-Zawra', please do not come here.
Baghdad is no longer a refuge; no one is here anymore.

The crown of the caliphate, the great monuments,
all has been burned to ashes.

Sa'di Shirazi (1219–94)

[A Bird in a Falcon's Grip]

I kept close my eyelids to prevent tears flowing;
when they overflowed, the dam could not stop them.

If only after the destruction, Baghdad's eastern breeze
had blown over my grave!

Death for true men
is prized, not a life of sorrow.

I scolded a physician who felt my pulse to treat me:
Stop it! I do not complain of any physical sickness.

While taking my leave, I was still patient,
but patience cannot cure my departure's malady.

If only I had died before Time's calamities;
if only I had not witnessed the wise man attacked by
    fools.

Afterward, inkwells wept with their blackness;
the hearts of some people are blacker than ink.

May God curse he who is dealt with kindness
and yet betrays when people attack.

Oh you who advise me to be patient, please leave me with
    my sighs!
With my heart tortured, can I be patient?

Crying without stop, my figure has been destroyed;
even mountains are destroyed when cleft apart.

I stood in Abadan looking into the Tigris —
like red blood flowing to the sea.

Do not ask me what the separation has done to my heart;
the wounds in my heart cannot be known by probing.

Muhammad's religion, says tradition,
will become strange again just as it was at the beginning.[61]

Could it be any stranger? Could Islam be as at the start?
Will the house of peace be occupied by infidels?

At the water's edge frogs play gladly;
can I be patient while Jonah rests at the bottom of the sea?

Crows crowd around the remains;
the 'Anqa'[62] stays in its nest.

---

61. According to a canonical Prophetic tradition, Muhammad said: "Islam
began strange, and it will become strange again just like it was at the
beginning." According to interpretations, "Islam will shrink back to the
Hijaz like the snake shrinks back into its hole."

62. The pre-Islamic mythological equivalent of the phoenix, a huge,
mysterious bird originally created by God as perfect in every way.

I wish my ears could have been deaf before they heard
how women's honor in captivity was violated.

They ran barefoot from desert to desert;
they were so tender, they could not walk on a bridge.

By your life, had you seen them on the night of their flight,
it was as if virgins were stars falling into darkness.

That morning, when the captives were led away, it was like
the Day of Judgment, the ingathering of the dead.

A cry is heard: Oh lost sense of honor, help!
But who would help a bird in a falcon's grip?

They were led like sheep in the desert's midst,
noble women unused to being chided.

They were dragged away, their breasts raised, their faces
    unveiled,
driven out from their private abodes.

I heard news that enraged my heart;
I carry misfortunes that weigh upon my back.

My heart, fragile as delicate glass,
a glass that cannot be mended.

My friend, truly life is so magnificent,
life is so wonderful; if only death does not come
    instantaneously.

Shams al-Din Muhammad ibn 'Abd
Allah al-Kufi (1226–76)

[Kings and Slaves]

I seek steadfastness, but my heart does not obey;
how could he whose thigh has betrayed him arise?

As if you had lost a friend, please share my mourning,
insofar as all are party to it.

Oh, what a catastrophe! No one saved himself from its
calamities; kings and slaves are equal.

After all the glory, the enemy defeated our beloved;
They left nothing; nothing remains.

If what afflicted our beloved could be ransomed,
I would do so with the very essence of my heart, with all I
    own.

Afterward, the haven of righteousness became
paralyzed; Islam's blood had been shed.

Where are those who have ruled all mankind?
Where are those who owned? Where are those who control?

The worn out remains, the deserted abodes, answer me:
Indeed, they were once here, but they have perished.

Shams al-Din Mahmud ibn Ahmad al-Hashimi al-Hanafi
(thirteenth century)

[*Stars to Be Followed*]

If my tears had not wounded my eyelids
after your departure, I would be a cruel person.

Since our separation, my eye's pupil has
not been content to gaze upon any other.

I wish I could have died before we split asunder;
I wish God had not kept me alive to witness separation.

Why have Time's calamities smashed
me, leaving me without friends?

What happened to the houses? Their occupants
are not my folks, the neighbors are not mine.

Believe me, after you departed, no one lived there except
seepage, destruction, and burning.

After you left, I visited the house
standing there confused.

I questioned it, but without words;
it spoke, but without a tongue.

I cried: Oh house, what have they done, those
who were the targets in their homeland?

Where are the people I knew? Because of their glory,
crowns used to bow down to them in humility.

They were stars to be followed; for their sake
justice and religion weep.

They fled, the house replied. When they dispersed,
humiliation substituted for glory.

Like the blood in veins spilling from the most noble place
into the most contemptible.

Time's calamities have destroyed them
as it destroyed the master of the palace.[63]

I watched the house after they left;
it was without occupants.

I still weep for them,
kissing the ruined sides of their camel's watering troughs.

Even strangers start to pity me,
those who do not know my love and sorrow.

---

63. The palace of Khosrau (531–79), twentieth Sassanid Emperor of Persia, a
monument in al-Mada'in and the only visible remaining structure of the
ancient city of Ctesiphon. It is near the modern town of Salman Pak, Iraq.

I wonder if the same house will ever bring us
together as we were, happy and joyous?!

We hasten to use time and pick,
with confident hands, the fruits of all hopes.

Fate's calamities serve us;
time helps us overcome the aggression.

Oh, gathering became impossible; Time's
calamities have blocked all ways to visit.

Why do I keep looking around, and I do not see
people from among the community of friends?

Oh my sorrow! Oh my loneliness! Oh my confusion!
Oh my solitude! Oh my aching warm heart!

Since you left, the breeze has not blown,
flowers have not bloomed, willow branches have not stirred.

My only companions, after you departed, are tears,
mourning, sorrow, and pain.

I wish I knew where your camels have gone,
where on earth is the place of your settling.

[Vow of Fidelity]

Because you left, I have pains;
how long will I be reproached by you and scolded?

Whoever left his beloved like me,
please do not scold him, for words can wound.

What a wonderful friend are the tears on my
cheek, but this friend slanders.

When a dove weeps, it melts my soul,
as if weeping were death.

If you lost a friend as I did,
if you have love and agony in your heart,

Please stand before the beloved's house and shout:
"Oh house, what has time done to you?"

I deserted you because, since my beloved has left,
"no smile can be seen on your face."[64]

Oh house, where are your dwellers?
Where reside glory and honor?

Oh house, where are the days of your elegance and
    kindness,

---

64. The second hemistich of the previous verse and this hemistich are
together the first verse of Abu Nuwas's poem in praise of al-Amin.

when your slogans were greatness and respectfulness?

Oh house, by God, since your stars have set,
darkness has covered us after the light.

They are far away; death is approaching;
the right path has been lost; Islam is shaken.

Why did you accept an enemy as a dweller
after the lover? May clouds never rain upon you.

Oh people, the heart longs
and shivers; my tears flow.

The house has lost your beautiful faces;
there is no room to stay inside.

Eyes have no luck in its courts,
neither have feet any access there.

By your life, I will remain faithful to love;
our bond has not been betrayed.

If I desire other than you, my blood may be shed;
life after you is forbidden.

Oh absent people, they are distant;
the fire burns between the ribs.

Your letters do not arrive; your news
is not retold; dreams do not bring you close.

You have rendered life horrible for me; whenever
you are far away, maladies have played with me.

Because of Time's injustice, I have encountered
things that I had never imagined.

I wish I could learn how my loved ones are;
where have they gone and settled?

I have no friend except just one verse,
by a lover stricken by arrows of separation:

"By God, I never chose separation;
that is Time's sentence on me."

Abu al-Khayr 'Abd al-Rahman Zayn al-Din al-Suwaydi
(1722–86)

[Tears and Weeping]

Without you, Oh city of al-Zawra', without longing for you
nothing would burn my heart.

May the rain water the surface of your earth;
may the generous clouds bless your face.

May your quarters be green even without spring;
may the flowers not vanish in your summer and winter.

Stop! I say to the tears flowing from my eyes,
to save your earth from their flood.

What a difference between Baghdad and Jillaq[65]
despite my bad luck, but my lot is only tears and weeping.

My hopes to meet you will never vanish,
I entertain them to myself.

Oh, Oh, I will never stop moaning
as long as I bewail my separation from you.

---

65. Damascus.

'Abd al-Ghani al-Jamil (1780–1863)

[Complaint]

Passing my eyes over Iraq, all I notice
among people is their hatred and enmity.

They are nice to strangers, cruel
toward one another, pretending all is fine.

Is there no one to lead people away from error,
to guide them on the most exalted path?!

Is there no man to save people from injustice,
when in wartime they need him to gore enemies with his
    horns?!

Though I am her child and suckling,
she has rejected me; may God never rain on her!

[Inner Storm]

Why stay in a city
where we are treated like asses?

Why not move to another place
to be honored and comforted?

May God not bless a city
where lions are considered sheep.

Every day she shows us only misfortunes;
every day she attacks us with sorrows.

If a city rejects its landlord,
then abandon her and she will crumble into nothingness.

I try — there is no relief;
my people are lazy, my illness, old age.

I call — nobody listens.
Can the deaf hear?

How long shall we remain quiet about evildoers?
How long shall we treat them as honorable?

I no longer belong in al-Karkh,
nor in al-Rusafa, the Persians' place.

A noble man is lost there,
while a wretch is honored.

Oh Mother, let me wander in the desert,
I swear upon your life, I have high aims.

You know I am a man
who never yields to oppression.

[*Once Glory Nested Here*]

My condolences for Baghdad, what a town!
Once glory nested here; now, it has flown away.

She was a bride like the morning's sun;
her jewels were not to be lent.

An abode for warrior lions,
a sanctuary for frightened fugitives.

Alas, no refuge now for the needy.
Her people offer no shelter.

The newcomers are blind,
knowing not good from evil.

While the lion disappears into the forest,
the bull is now the chief master.

Prosperous trade has perished;
Baghdad is a present-day hell.

On her fences owls perch wailing:
What a wreck! What a wreck!

Al-Karkh is deserted by its people;
they were a fragrant species.

Her name is al-Zawra';[66] —
she strayed from the straight way.

Her people have no shame;
scoundrels commit injustices; noble people are bewildered.

All here strike sparks;
the start of a fire is only a spark.

The rage of a man with honor
will not be satisfied with no blade.

Oh Shihab al-Din, Oh my master,
rogues attack us and spread injustice.

Monkeys have become the leaders there;
they gamble with human hearts.

---

66. *Zawra'* in Arabic also means cross-eyed woman.

Shihab al-Din Abu al-Thana' Mahmud al-Alusi
(1803–54)

[*Longing and Craving*][67]

Suddenly, a great longing for al-Zawra' struck me;
what they told me about her is not simple.

If people of the City of Peace cannot stay there,
there is no longer a mountain or valley to shelter
  noblemen.

If the shadow offered by the city diminishes,
how can we find any shelter in the desert?!

If the pure water in her soil dwindles,
what drink in other places can be sweet for us?!

That was a place where I felt protected;
that was my home where roots and branches grew.

That was a place where I lived; my she-camel thrived on
  her fertile soil;
my he-camel was satisfied; my assets grew.

I wonder, will I live once again in that
abode? Will I meet again those I love?

---

67. While staying in Istanbul, the poet longed for his children and yearned
for his homeland.

Will her gardens bloom again after they have withered?
Will drops of dew once again linger on leaves?

On Friday will I be on my way
to the al-Kaylani Mosque, to the assembly of loved ones.

Will I again hold the hand of my father,
Abu Mustafa, a man of endless ambitions?

Will men of letters from both banks meet me
in an assembly of blossoming culture?

Peace be upon those places and people;
wherever they stay, they are always in my heart.

I swear by God, I cannot find any substitute for her air and
    water;
my heart is there; how can I find consolation?

Oh my loved ones, is there any chance to meet again?
The messengers between us became weary.

No distraction weakens my resolve to be with you;
if you so desire, our ties will be restored.

Even if you do wrong,
the bitterness of it is all sweet to me.

'Abd al-Ghaffar al-Akhras al-Mawsili (1805–72)

[*Peace Be with Baghdad*]

Peace be with Baghdad! Once she gave me peace of mind;
farewell from a bored man, not bored to say goodbye.

Paying no heed, I will desert Baghdad
to join the already departed.

To the many complaints, I say, relax,
while something whispers in my heart.

If people do not know my worthiness,
I will show them my power.

How can I stay among these boors?
They cannot discern gold from brass.

Radi al-Qazwini (1819–68)

[Baghdad and Tibriz]

My beloved people in al-Zawra' of Iraq,
we have been apart for too long; when will we meet?

Tibriz is not a refuge for eloquent Arabic speakers.
Could you ever compare Turks to the Arabs of Iraq?

'Abd al-Hamid al-Shawi (1828–98)

[*I Remember Baghdad*]⁶⁸

I remembered Baghdad while relaxing
in Najd and its plains.

I remember Baghdad neither because I love her
nor because of the friendship of her denizens.

I remember her because of her leaders,
kings of the earth, the ornaments of her crown.

What benefit to live in a city
that repudiates us after long acquaintance?

As if we were not expelled from her borders,
while Persian armies escaped to their countries,

With swords whose blows hastened
the farewells that heads gave to their bodies.

If we had not defended her, female prisoners
would have been sold at low prices.

---

68. While the poet was spending time in Najd, he composed these verses in
which he expressed his pride in his ancestors, who helped defeat the Iranians
when they tried to occupy Baghdad. He reproached those who had not
sufficiently appreciated the deeds of Baghdad's residents.

In Baghdad, we encountered only frigidity
and injustice — no humans were there.

The best of her nobility are mistreated
while the lowest of her slaves are revered.

The hearts of the generous are sullied
by one-eyed and blind monkeys.

There is nothing good about her old people;
her youth are ugly and poor.

All are equal in bad habits —
like donkeys' teeth.

Ahmad al-Shawi (1844–99)

[Memory]

Between al-Rusafa and the bridge I remember
happy days of childhood that my heart longs to recall.

Longing has returned, forgetting
happiness; a new ember has pierced my heart.

Friends, will days of youth return
along with my al-Karkh? What wonderful days they were!

The horses of ignorance approach,
pleasures and desires without constraints.

Each young man accorded immorality what it deserved,
wine according to desire.

How we urged the bartender,
insisting on wine and much more.

Arrogantly trailing our garments,
as though we were kings proudly dragging our trains.

Oh my reproacher, if you want to heap blame upon me,
wait, please wait, for reproach only degrades.

I beg you, do not continue your reproach;
you know I have had enough.

If man's soul does not reject immoral acts,
then why is a nobleman considered noble?

If old age does not stop man from indulging in
pleasures and desires, then he is worthless.

[Leaders]

Don't you see? Misery or happiness of a place,
all depends on its leaders.

Like people, at times a place is humiliated,
at other times it is glorified and revered.

Many a sick country we have seen,
that lions cured them by wise means.

Many a country has been cured only
to be made sick again by a terrible leader.

May Baghdad's square be a lesson for all,
as anyone who speaks the truth must admit.

Jamil Sidqi al-Zahawi (1863–1936)

[*Baghdad Days*]

Baghdad days, will they return to
Baghdad, after separation and dissolution?

Baghdad days, even the bitter ones,
transcended the trials of time, never yielded.

Baghdad was not the city you see today;
her rulers were not oppressive.

She was an abode for sciences and scientists,
a foundation for glory and creativity.

Today all knowledge is buried
in the graves of the forefathers.

Once her residents lived in paradise;
that paradise is lost.

Those were days protected by shade,
a paradise for her visitors.

Baghdad days are shining, beautiful,
glittering like stars.

Will her demolished edifice rise again,
or is there no longer any hope?

For all our desires to be realized,
just as souls do not return to corpses,

If only righteous rule would return,
if only the regime of wrongs would be removed.

(1908)[69]

[*Behind Bars*]

In Baghdad, I was never at peace.
In Baghdad, I was never happy.

Singing to others from behind bars,
surviving off mere crumbs.

I saw a life of humiliation spreading;
people are happy or sad.

Life offers many different paths;
in each place, people take a different one.

---

69. Written on the Ottoman Constitution of 1908.

[*Migration*]

Your stay in al-Zawra' is undesirable;
your kindness toward enemies is of no use.

Your wishes in its nights are foolish;
your opinions of its days are unwise.

I will leave Baghdad a frustrated man;
too long have I lived in a house of humiliation.

I will abandon my family, desert my homeland;
I will cut off all ties, past and present.

I have never seen a place like Baghdad,
where knowledge is met with stinginess.

I was miserable there, happy too, but
I found no relief from envy or gloating.

I struggled days and nights;
they beat me black and white.

Ahmad Shawqi (1868–1932)

[Baghdad and Rome]

Forget Rome and Athens and all that they contain.
All jewels are only in Baghdad.

At the mention of the Abode of Peace, the Abode of Law,
    Rome,
hastens to congratulate her.

When they meet, Rome cannot equal her in eloquence.
In a court of law, she cannot challenge her rival.

Among Rome's emperors you will never find
the likes of al-Rashid, al-Ma'mun, and al-Mu'tasim.[70]

They are people of knowledge and science,
unchallenged in wisdom and intellect.

When they utter a single word, scholars bow
not with deference to the ruler, but out of respect for
    science.

---

70. During the golden age of the caliphs of Baghdad in the eighth and ninth centuries, Al-Rashid (reigned 786–809), al-Ma'mun (reigned 813–33), and al-Mu'tasim (reigned 833–42) were among the most famous and successful caliphs.

Hafiz Ibrahim (1871–1932)

[*Tenderness and Gentleness*]

In Harun al-Rashid's time we reached the skies;
people lived in harmony.

Learning adorned every neck;
our conduct was shaped by tenderness and gentleness.

Ask what place on earth could be compared
to Baghdad under Islam.

Her people, never weak in the face of calamities;
her learning, upholding the Qur'an.

Ma'ruf al-Rusafi (1875–1945)

[*The Bridge*]⁷¹

As if al-Zawra' were a young woman, the bridge
on her thin waist like a belt.

Like a necklace of pearls on
the neck of the river.

Al-Rusafa longed for al-Karkh,
extending a hand to touch her.

(Baghdad, 1902)

[*The Flood*]⁷²

Oh Baghdad, enough of slumber and sleep;
do these catastrophes never trouble you?

Misery has fallen in love with you;
no doctors can cure your maladies.

Time is now hostile.
Can you avenge yourself?

---

71. Written on the occasion of the opening of the Baghdad Bridge in 1902.

72. In 1907 three rivers overflowed: Tigris, Euphrates, and Dayali. The dams on the rivers collapsed, the water covered al-Karkh, and al-Rusafa was inundated by the water. These verses are from a poem written after the catastrophe.

I wonder why injustice should afflict you,
as if patrons had never nurtured you?

From Dayali, Euphrates, and Tigris,
troubles plague your people.

Three rivers flowing with life,
yet the earth around you is barren.

Your people have lost their minds.
How can a nation be rightly guided by ignorant leaders?

The nation has lost its glory and fallen apart.
You see a group, yet they are merely fragments.

Here is al-Rusafa encircled by water;
al-Karkh is ridden with calamities too.

The waters of the two rivers have overflowed,
sweeping away the fragile dams.

The Euphrates has united with the Tigris;
valleys and hills have become as one.

Flood's armies kept advancing.
They fell upon al-Karkh with a mighty uproar.

As they streamed onto houses with noxious fluids,
the houses spat out their residents.

Al-Karkh now becomes a scene of misery;
young men and women weep.

Roads are closed, houses destroyed,
courtyards are filthy.

Who would notify al-Mansur[73] about his Baghdad,
with news that makes us weep?

Where are the towers that you built so high?
Where are the palaces with lofty balconies?

Where are the gardens, the rivers beneath them?
Where are the fruit-laden trees?

Where are the days when justice shone its light,
when wisdom's flags flew high above you?

When civilization was at its zenith like
the moon, you were haloed with paeans of praise?

When learning sang its songs,
you used to grant them gifts?

When noble people addressed you,
you gave gifts in profusion?

A time when a petulant man would present his case
and still depart relaxed?

---

73. The caliph who founded Baghdad.

Months would pass, amicably;
hours would pass, smiling.

What disgrace disfigures you now?
Your signs of glory have been erased.

Why do rivers hurt you instead of being
a source of goodness and life?

(Baghdad, 1907)

Oh Lover of the Orient!

Oh lover of the Orient,
Welcome, Mr. Craine.

You have come, Mr. Craine.
So take a look and see the East.

It is a prisoner of the West,
like a debtor to a creditor.

The East here, the West there —
deceived and deceiver.

If you were to ask what is
going on in Baghdad

It is a regime whose udder is oriental —
the milk is English.

National in name —
yet English in nature.

Arabian but alien,
Arabized in language, but still gibberish.

In this regime, the significant secret —
orders come from London.

It is double-faced,
the visible dependent on the cryptic.

In outward appearance, we
rule everything.

But in essence we
do nothing.

Is this what goes on in your West,
Oh Mr. Craine?!

(Baghdad, 1929)[74]

---

74. Poet's note: "Recited at a big celebration held by the National Party in
Baghdad in honor of Mr. Craine, the famous rich American, on the occasion
of his visit to Baghdad in 1929."

Iliyya Abu Madi (1889–1957)

When Fate Came Knocking

If ever a man on earth could live forever,
Harun al-Rashid would never have died, Mu'awiya[75]
    would be alive even today.

If glory could be everlasting, Baghdad would never have
    become collapsed ruins.
Yet catastrophes struck her; her houses became ruins.

Storm winds knocked them down; now owls live there;
nothing scares them; ravens dwell in rubble.

When Fate came knocking, the very walls that defeated
violent armies could not protect her.

---

75. Mu'awiya ibn Abi Sufyan (602–680), the first caliph of the Umayyad
Dynasty.

Anwar Sha'ul (1904–84)

[Happy in Baghdad]

From Moses I borrowed my creed,
but under Muhammad's faith I have long lived.

Islam's generosity was my shelter;
Qur'an's eloquence was my fountain.

My adherence to Moses's creed
diminished not my love for Muhammad's nation.

Faithful I will stay like al-Samaw'al[76]
whether happy in Baghdad or miserable.

(Baghdad, February 1969)

---

76. Al-Samaw'al ibn 'Adiya' was a pre-Islamic Jewish poet, proverbial in Arabic ancient heritage for his loyalty.

[Love of the Arabs]

My heart beats with love of the Arabs,
my mouth proudly speaks their tongue.

Do they and I not share a common source?
The distant past drew us together.

That day in al-Ablaq, when al-Samaw'al incorporated
in the book of faithfulness an Arab example.

Today we march toward glory;
together we long for a happy tomorrow.

My childhood blossomed by the waters of the Tigris.
The days of my youth drank of the Euphrates.

Oh Homeland of Arabism, blessed be you as a shelter
whose beauty shines throughout the country.

I love my dear homeland and those
who ennobled me with their love.

Our fates have been bound together in a homeland,
which is water, air, and glamor to us.

(*Baghdad, April 1969*)

Murad Michael (1906–86)

Oh My Fatherland! (Excerpts)

Oh my fatherland, Oh my fatherland!
Your love has enslaved me!

Your love is the object of my desire!
You are my father and mother!

Oh my fatherland! Oh my fatherland!

Oh my fatherland, you are hope!
You are my mind and intellect.

You are the best abode,
my support when calamities hit me

Oh my fatherland! Oh my fatherland!

My heart has fallen in love with you.
My heart rebelled against loving you.

By God, if there is no cure,
cure my agony by uniting lovers.

Oh my fatherland! Oh my fatherland!

How many nights did I sleep
with only sleeplessness as my share!

I am watching the constellations in the skies
on the carpet of sorrow!

Oh my fatherland! Oh my fatherland!

My soul is your ransom, Oh my fatherland!
Be at peace; do not be afraid of any trials!

Today, your soil is my abode;
tomorrow your soil will embrace my corpse.

Oh my fatherland! Oh my fatherland!

(*Baghdad, April 11, 1922*)

Mir Basri (1911–2006)

[*Oh Friends of Life!*]

Oh friends of life! Even as my death draws near,
please bury me in the safety of the wide land.

Near my ancestors who slept for ages
in Baghdad's soil — this is the beloved mother.

Let me rest in the shadow of palm dates,
where dreams of youth will overflow the eyelids.

I will remember life, which passed away;
I will forget the painful nights.

Oh friends of love, my youth passed by
like flowers withered while still wet.

Oh Baghdad, Oh refuge for my love,
Oh shelter for my soul and close home.

Life was delightful, pleasant;
how could hard hours not be sweet.

When you wronged, it was justice;
when you envied, it was good.

Oh homeland, you are my happiness and misery;
you are my malady, my remedy, and healer.

Oh homeland, a place of goodness and beauty,
good manners and fortunate spirit.

Fortress of noble-hearted men, rejecting wrongdoing,
stable glory and strong spirit.

I am one of them, I do not want any alternative
nor any other homeland.

She is my cradle, where my life dawned.
When the time comes, I will die there.

(October 13, 1950)

Mishil Haddad (1919–96)

The Books

Hulagu[77] will come and burn the books,
Before eyes grow feeble,
Before ideas are muddled,
Before their crowded languages teach us
Tranquility,
Before that,
He will come!

(1985)

---

77. Destroyer of Baghdad in 1258.

Nizar Qabbani (1923–98)

A Baghdadi Song

Please spread for me a carpet, fill my glasses,
forget the blame, I have forgotten yours.

Your eyes, Oh Baghdad, since childhood,
two suns sleeping in my eyelashes.

Don't reject my face, you are my beloved,
the flowers on my desk, my wine glass as well.

Baghdad, I come as worn out as a ship
hiding my wounds beneath my clothes.

I threw my head on my princess's breast;
our lips met after long absence.

I am that very sailor who lost his life,
searching for love and lovers.

Baghdad, I have flown on a silky cloak,
on the plaits of Zaynab and Rabab.[78]

I have landed like a bird eager to reach its nest;
the dawn is a marriage of minarets and domes.

---

78. Names of two beloved women that classical Arabic poets used to
mention in their poems.

Until I saw you, a jewel
resting amidst vineyards and palms.

Wherever I turned, I saw my homeland's traits,
wafting in the earth, my earth.

I have never left you; in every blue
cloud you will find the pride of my clouds.

The stars dwelling on your hills
are the very same stars that inhabit my hills.

Baghdad, I have experienced beauty in all its colors, but
your beauty was unimaginable.

What could I write about you in the books of love?
For love of you, a thousand books are not enough!

My poetry assassinates me; every poem
sucks me dry, sips the oil of my youth.

The golden dagger drinks from my blood,
sleeps in my flesh and nerves.

Baghdad, you aria of bracelets and jewels,
Oh treasure of lights and perfumes.

Do not harm the fiddle string in my hand,
for desire is greater than my hand and the fiddle.

Before the sweet encounter, you were my beloved.
You will remain after I leave.

(Baghdad, March 8, 1962)

Glory to the Long Plaits

. . . once upon a time in Baghdad, Oh my beloved, there
    was
A caliph; his daughter was beautiful,
Her eyes —
Two green birds,
Her hair, a long poem.
Many a king and emperor approached her
With bridal presents:
Caravans of slaves and gold,
Presenting their crowns on
Golden platters.
From India came a prince,
From China came silk,
But the beautiful princess
Rejected the king, the palaces, and the jewels.
She desired a poet
Who every evening would throw
A flower onto her balcony,
A charming word.

So tells us Shahrazad:
. . . and the cruel caliph took vengeance and
  Cut the plaits,
  Plait after plait,

And Baghdad, Oh my beloved, declared mourning
No less than two years,
And Baghdad, Oh my beloved, declared mourning,
On yellow golden spikes.
The land became hungry.
Not even one spike in the granaries,
Trembled,
Not even a single grape.
The malicious caliph,
His mind and heart of wood,
Announced a reward of a thousand dinars for the head of
    the poet.
He sent his soldiers to burn
All flowers in the palace,
All plaits in Iraq.

Oh my beloved, time will erase
This same caliph.
His life will come to an end
Like any other clown.
Glory to you, Oh my beautiful princess!
In your eyes, two green birds were asleep.
Glory will remain for the long plaits,
For the charming word.

(1966)

Nazik al-Mala'ika (1923–2007)

The Passionate River[79]

Where can we go? The river rushes toward us,
Running across wheat fields, never slowing its steps,
With the glow of dawn spreading its arms for us,
Leaping in ecstasy, like the wind, its hands
Will touch us and contain our horror wherever we go.

The river rushes and rushes,
Crossing our villages, soundlessly.
Its muddy water sweeps away; no dam can stop it.
It pursues us, yearning to contain our youth
In its arms and spread upon us its love.

The river still pursues us, smiling lovingly,
Its wet feet
Leaving their red traces in every place.
It has tenderly ravaged
East and West.

Where can we escape after the river
Envelops the city's shoulders?
It acts slowly and silently but firmly,
It pours forth from its lips
Muddy kisses that immerse our sad farmland.

---

79. Written during the flood that hit Baghdad in 1954.

That lover, we knew it before;
It never ceased crawling toward our hills.
For its sake we built, developing our villages as well.
It was an unusual guest, yet generous;
Every year it flowed into the valley and came to meet us.

We have evacuated our huts under cover of night,
We will take shelter and go.
Yet it pursues us everywhere.
We pray for it.
Faced with it we complain about our boring life.

Now the river has become a god.
Haven't our buildings washed their feet in its water?
It rises and pours its treasures in front of them.
It grants us mud and invisible death.
And now what is left for us?
Now, what has remained for us?

(1954)

Ibrahim Ovadia (1924–2006)

A Guest in Tehran[80]

He said to me: "You left your homeland moving
from one country to another.

You left Baghdad while she was stormy,
and came back while she was on a volcano's mouth.

Today, you are far away again, after departing from her;
two years have passed.

Has she been blown up with her dwellers,
or has she become devoid of all conscience?"

Bitter and sorrowful, I responded:
"With memories, you arouse my agony;

I am not alone; many children of my homeland
escaped to Iran along with their suffering too.

In their exile, they are my family;
in our loss, we are all brothers.

---

80. In 1948, the poet left Baghdad for Tehran of his own free will and
returned in October 1949. In the meantime, an anti-Jewish atmosphere was
developing in Baghdad following the establishment of the State of Israel. In
the beginning of 1951, the poet left again for Tehran, this time unwillingly and
for good. From Tehran he immigrated to Israel, where he lived until his death.

Our roots in Iraq were planted,
but we now live in Tibriz or Shemiran.[81]

Like me, they found refuge in Iran
but, am I in Iran Iranian?

I have never changed my identity while living
in a place remote from or close to the land of the two
    rivers.

I am the son of Baghdad, whenever you meet me.
I am the son of Baghdad, wherever you see me.

But Baghdad, I mean her attitude,
made me a guest in Tehran!"

(Tehran, 1951)

---

81. Shemiran is a neighborhood of Tehran.

'Ali Sidqi 'Abd al-Qadir (1924–2008)

Baghdad and the Black Eyes

I sailed into the eyes of Baghdad, setting my sail for
Islands whose plants are love, poetry, and longing.
At my fingers tips the fragrance of those eyes,
The smell of apple,
And a horse-bell's sigh.

I stood, while children were playing in Baghdad,
Jumping on the sun fence,
Creating tiny balls of its rays,
Planting the seed of life.

We were three:
Me, Baghdad, and twin eyes.
A door opened in our sun; everyone watched.
Our land rained honey, milk, and carnelians.
We were three playing with carnelians and empty
    glasses,
Till we curled up and slept on the lock of scent.
When we got exhausted,
The day removed its shoe, its strides not rousing those
    asleep.
Walking quietly, shoes in hand,
It scooped up stars — they were all still asleep,
Scooping them up one after another,
Walking along alleys with pierced ears
To place earrings in the lobes.

We were three: Me, Baghdad, and twin eyes,
And a Baghdadi woman's mouth about whom my story is
    long,
For which my fate rests
To the end of time
And will never cease.
Her cheek was no farther away from me than a birthmark
    and a song,
And five whispers, her earring,
The tremor of dimples when she smiled.
A shadow of a laugh saying yes, no,
And a magic word never ending,
Starting with *Lo* and ending with *ve*.
What separates us is a thin thread,
It is the beginning of the road,
One with no end.

Night in Baghdad slept in black eyes,
On a bright meandering horse,
I spent the night coloring an apple and some figs.
There I was born multiple times;
I lived a thousand lives.
After drinking rivers, I was still thirsty.
I danced through the night, incessantly
Dancing in my blood, the way of God.
We were three: Me, Baghdad, and twin eyes.

(*2007*)

Badr Shakir al-Sayyab (1926–64)

Death the Fox[82]

How it grates the heart that men should become the
    hunter's prey just like gazelles; as helpless as sparrows,
Cowering, trembling with fright, shaking in panic, be-
    cause a fearsome shadow falls slowly, Oh so slowly.
Death the Fox, Death the Horseman, Izra'il approaches,
    whetting his blade. Ah!
He grits his hungry teeth and glares threateningly. Oh my
    God, if only life could be oblivion
Before this oblivion, this end;
If only this end might be a beginning.
Oh gruesome agony! Did children's eyes but see this
    destroyer, menacing, dying his hands in blood, with
    fire in his eyes and between his jaws,
How their hands would twitch, how they would rush for
    shelter,
As he draws ever closer . . . as though stirring up a wind,
Destroying,
Destroying, menacing, destroying.
Those who have witnessed a rustic hen when evening
    comes to the yard, when the ravenous fox slinks toward
    it — just hear its teeth grind — it stands there shaking,
    paralyzed by fear, riveted to its death spot; as though
    the paths . . .

---

82. Translated by Roger Allen.

Have been snatched away by some ogre, as though those
    teeth
Were the Baghdad wall with the gates closed, no escape
    and no salvation.
That is how we are when Izrail the hunter comes:
Convulsions, then murder.

(1960)

Brothel

Baghdad is a gigantic brothel
(The female singer Lawahiz
Like a clock ticking on the wall
In the sitting hall of a train station).
Oh thou corpse lying on the earth,
The worms eat it — a wave of fire and silk.

Baghdad is a nightmare
(A corrupted ruin imbibed by the somnolent,
Its hours are days, its days years, the year a yoke,
The year a seething wound in the heart).

"Does' eyes between al-Rusafa and the bridge" —
Bullet-holes decorating the face of the full moon.
On Baghdad the moon pours down
A cascade of ashes from both eyes' sockets:
All the houses are a single house,
All roads are squeezed, like threads,
Into one rebellious fist

Stretching away and crippling,
Making them a road into a midday heat.
The faces of all beautiful girls are the face of Nahida
(My beloved whose saliva is honey,
My little girl, her buttocks hills,
Her breasts, summits).

In Baghdad we are a clay
That the potter soaks into a statue,
A world for dreams of madmen.
We are colors on her shaking gulf, corpses, and limbs.

Yesterday there was a festival, the festival of roses:
The provisions scattered by hills, wines as well,
Dances and songs,
Love and sounds of laughter.
Then everything ended save for the remaining birds
Pecking at seeds, save for blood
The field had grown — the bird is the informer —
Save for children wandering in the city of Ur:
"This is the festival — who said our festival has ended?
Let's fill the world with our songs,
The earth still rotates by festivals,
Yesterday there was a festival, the festival of roses
And today? What will we do today?
Shall we sow or kill?"

Is this Baghdad?
Or has Gomorrah returned
And the hereafter has come as death?

And I resound with chains.
I felt . . . what? The sound of the noria
Or the cry of sap in the roots?

(1960)[83]

Because I Am a Stranger

Because I am a stranger
Because my dear Iraq
Is far away, I am here longing
For her. "Iraq," I cry!
But my cry comes back as weeping
Bursting out of the echo.
I feel I have traversed the distance
To a world of death, not responding
To my cry.
When I shake the branches
Only death falls.
Stones,
Stones, not fruit,
Even eyes are
Stones, even the wet air,
Stones moistened by drops of blood,
Stones are my cry; rock is my mouth.
My legs are wind as they wander across deserts.

(April 15, 1962)

---

83. Poet's note: "This poem was written during the bygone period [of monarchy] before the revolution of 1958."

Buland al-Haydari (1926–96)

On the Way of Exile from Baghdad

Baghdad chases me,
Besieges me,
From all the mirror's corners.
She presses me to exile, accused of cowardice,
Because
I was afraid for my face of my eyes.
That is why I swore I would gouge out my eye.
I would turn off my mirror
Lest I see my coming face
Escaping from me,
And because
I cut my tongue into pieces,
I nailed my dumbness
On the long black walls
And the homeland's prisons' fortifications,
Because I swore before all guards
To be more the coward than my homeland,
More the coward asking what they have done to my
     homeland
More the coward to ask what. . . ?
— Say it! Say it!
What have they left of my homeland,
Except graves pregnant with rottenness.

[*Three lines omitted by the censor*][84]

---

84. In the original.

I beg your pardon, Baghdad,
If I come to you mutilated, dumb,
Poorer than the desert's nakedness,
More miserable than the desert's sand.
The border guards of the detestable homeland have
    stripped me
Even of my flesh and skin,
Even of my dream to be born in the wound,
To prevent me from growing in the dagger.
They cut off all the ten fingers of my hands
And, to be safe, they cut off as well
All the ten toes of my feet.
And I did not know
Why the greater homeland's border guard granted me
A broken pen and both covers of a notebook!

[*Three lines omitted by the censor*][85]

Oh black earth colored with malady,
If I come to you again,
Please close your doors before me, before the desert
And the desert's nakedness
And the desert's salt.
Keep the promise and the doubt.
Keep being a window which one day perhaps will
    summarize all my skies.

(*1990*)

---

85. In the original.

The City That Was Lost because of Her Silence

Troy, that forgotten female prisoner
Between the corpse and the nail.

Troy — the Greeks never besieged her;
The Persians never seduced her.
She has never been lured away by any storm or fire.

Troy died because of a wound inside her,
Because of a blind silence that tied her children's tongues.

That female prisoner was not a motherland;
She was only a prison,
Twisted with black walls and fences.
She was not a darkness after which dawn would rise.
Troy, that forgotten female prisoner
Was lost because of her silence.
Now she is only a desert where death alone dwells,
Befriended only by stones.

It was a time, when she was about to be one day
Something in secret,
No more than a secret murmured in a room's silence;
She was about to be a promise in the eyes,
A pledge of blue films.
We were about to live a dream inside her,
Paper boats borne by the stream, floating,
Waving, never asking about a port,
To be tied on any shore.
How much we wanted her to be a flash of

Lightning to reveal the desire,
But . . .

— Listen! Listen!
I listened; I pricked my ears, but
Heard nothing.
— Listen! Listen!

I laughed. That is a cat's voice in the neighbor's
    apartment;
It's only leaves rustling.
Pay no attention to them; it's only the cat,
Nothing but leaves rustling.

Suddenly, four knocks on the door.
The heart pounds for fear of a thousand knocks
— Listen! Don't you hear? Don't you notice?
I see a figure lying in wait behind the window,
In the darkness of his eyes, yes,
In the darkness of his eyes, I am about to see my weeping
    face.
Tomorrow the report will be prepared;
Tomorrow the rationale for killing you will be prepared.
Oh Troy, within us and because of us.
And we should approve it; we are the corpse and the nail,
While you are forgotten between the corpse and the nail.

— You all were awake till dawn.
— Yes, we were awake till dawn, but we . . .
— What does that mean? What does it suggest?
On the chair, two of its ribs were removed,

And on the black table,
Close to the lantern with its shimmering light,
There were white papers, others yellowish, puss-colored,
There was an open book as well,
Like an exposed secret,
And the remains of two pencils.
What does it mean that you read, that you write?
What does it mean that you were awake till dawn?
What does it mean? What does it suggest?

We will be executed in Troy Square.
On both our chests there will be a sign bigger than Troy.
You should know if you don't want to die, if you wish to
    live,
It is forbidden to read or write,
To speak or weep or even ask.
What does Troy mean?
What does it mean that you are a man or a beast,
Or you are more than a forgotten stone in Troy?
It is forbidden to be more than the legs of a whore,
Or the hands of a pimp.

Troy died because of a wound inside us, because of a
    wound inside her,
Because of a blind silence that tied her children's
    tongues.
Troy, the silence killed her.
We have nothing inside her; she has nothing inside us save
    death,
Nothing but the corpse and the nail.

(*London, February 1989*)

Apology

I beg your pardon
Oh you, our great guests,
I beg your pardon, Oh you, coming from the country's
    remotest parts.
The broadcaster has lied in his latest news bulletin.
There is neither sea in Baghdad,
Nor pearls or island.
All that al-Sindibad said
About queens of demons,
About islands of rubies and pearls,
About rivers carrying in their dreams
Ports
Harbors
Is nonsense, fairy tale of summer heat
In my small city
Where we had
Sea, sea shells and white pearls
Till resurrection and birth.

I beg your pardon.
There is nothing in Baghdad except her old walls,
Except her ugly silence,
Except the stars' exile in . . .
Her nights' silence
And except what has been left to her dreamers:
A vacant, blind paradise.
The broadcaster has lied in his latest news bulletin,
And a worm dreaming of living in our buried eyes.

And we, Oh you, coming from the country's remotest
    parts,
And we, Oh you, our dear great guests,
We lie in order to be reborn,
We lie down in order to remain in our long history
A story we will eschew in yellow books about . . .
About our ancient glory,
About our glorious glory,
A fairy tale related by al-Sindibad
Where we had sea shells and white pearls,
And a death that comes as a birth.

I beg your pardon.
I beg your pardon, Oh you, coming from the country's
    remotest parts.
I beg your pardon, Oh you, our great guests.
Baghdad has no sea, pearls or island
Nothing hides the sun of the small city
But our shadow and shame steeped in blackness
In a big lie,
Like sea, like pearls, like resurrection and birth
In a big lie called Baghdad.

                                                            (1993)

'Abd al-Wahhab al-Bayyati (1926–99)

A Sigh in Baghdad

I am searching for a cloud,
A green cloud that will wipe away my depression,
Will transport me
To my homeland's deserts,
To the lily fields
That will grant me
A butterfly and a star,
A water drop to quench my thirst and a word.
The Tigris waters were muddy
And only flowed
To flood dams and villages.
So, who would bathe me with his water and
Bury me under a palm tree's shadows?
Who, after a thousand years, would chant for me a verse?
My homeland is far away.
These dusky nights separate us,
Ink and papers as well,
And the wall of longings.
Oh Ma'arrat al-Nu'man,[86] garden of gold,
The summer came and left,
And you still laugh
Happily, playing in the sand.
The crow has landed on your balcony,
The beloveds have gone,

---

86. The birthplace of the poet Abu al-'Ala' al-Ma'arri (973–1058).

Dispersed like so many tribes.
The trees have dried,
Nightingales emigrated before noon.
Only death hovers over ruins and temples.
Only poetry remains in the ages' memory.
After one thousand years the grapes will ripen
And cups will be filled
And the singer will be revived.
Oh, Oh, my love and my sorrow!

(1965)

The City

1

When the city undressed herself,
I could see in her sad eyes
The shabbiness of leaders, thieves, and pawns.
I saw in her eyes erected gallows,
Prisons, and incinerators,
Sadness, confusion, and smoke.
I saw in her eyes, a human being,
Glued like a postage stamp
On everything.
I saw blood and crime,
Matchboxes and meat tins.
In her eyes I saw orphan childhood
Wandering, searching in garbage dumps
For a bone,
For a moon dying,
Upon the corpses of houses.

I saw the human being of tomorrow
Displayed in storefronts, on coins, and chimneys,
Clothed with blackness and sorrow,
Shackled, while the policeman,
The sodomite and pimp
Spit in his eyes.
In her sad eyes, I saw
Gardens of ashes
Drowned in shadow and tranquility.

2

When evening covered her nudity,
The silence enveloped her blind houses,
She sighed
And smiled despite the pallor of her sickness.
Her black eyes shone with goodness and purity.

(1969)

An Elegy to an Unborn City

Buzzing with people and flies,
I was born there; on her walls I knew alienation and
     wandering,
Love, death, and exile of poverty within her gates and
     underworld.
My father taught me to read rivers,
Fire, clouds, and mirage,
Rebellion, and perseverance.
He taught me to cruise the seas,
To grieve and circle

The houses of God's saints,
Searching for light and warmth of a future spring as yet
    not here,
Still living at the bottom of earth, in sea shells,
Awaiting a prophecy of the fortune-teller.
He taught me to wait for night and day,
To search on the world map for
A hidden, enchanted city,
Similar in the color of her eyes and sad laugh
But not garbed in the rags and tatters
Of a wandering clown.
Neither would her summer be abuzz with people and flies.

(1970)

Words on al-Sayyab's Tomb

I am climbing your walls, Baghdad, falling dead at night,
Straining my eyes to see your houses, smelling the interim
    flower,
Lamenting al-Husayn.[87]
I will be lamenting him till God unites the two separated
    lovers,
Demolishing the wall of separation.
And we will be meeting again as children
Beginning where things begin,
Watering thirsty butterflies,

---

87. Al-Husayn ibn 'Ali ibn Abi Talib (626–80) — son of 'Ali, the fourth
Islamic caliph, and Fatima, daughter of the Prophet Muhammad. He is
revered by Shiite Muslims as the third Imam.

Making fires of our notebooks,
Escaping into the gardens,
Writing love poems on the wall,
Painting gazelles and houris,
Dancing naked
Beneath lights of Iraq's moon
Shouting under al-Taq:[88]
Baghdad, Oh Baghdad, Oh Baghdad!
We have come to you from clay houses and tombs of ashes,
After death we will be destroying your walls,
We will be killing this night,
With screams of our love, crucified beneath the sun.

(1970)

A Profile of a City

A cemetery above a cemetery, between them
Love, death, living humans and
Beggars and stingy people of wealth.
If you shouted in your loudest voice,
The echo would come back full of gasps from the dead and
Coughs of winters of years past.
If you tried to flee,
Vendors, impostors, and tricksters would chase after you
In that big cemetery,
That very mill,
That very desert

---

88. Poet's note: "Al-Taq: Kisra palace near Baghdad, where we used to go when we were children, shouting beneath it, and it would echo all that we said."

Where gods of poetry were slaughtered.
And the poet died in the tavern.

(May 27, 1986)

Al-'Abbas ibn al-Ahnaf: Impossible Love[89]

1

Baghdad's taverns are lit.
Who will open the gate for me?
Al-'Abbas is sick and lonely.
Scared, he shut his eyes.
He saw a concubine dancing in a cup
And called her:
Are you the red flower in the river of madness?
Which slave-trader sold you in the market to Satan?
Here and now you are mine alone.
I will strip you of the heavenly inheritance
and the legacy of Mongol taverns.
So dance in the cup, Oh mistress of night,
And return to Bukhara and Samarkand,
And to the labyrinthine deserts of existence
As a child playing in her garden,
Picking the stars' flowers
While I rise from my death,
From Baghdad's taverns,
From the swamps of miserable life,
Bearing the sorrow of drunken singers
And the bequests of the deprived poor.

---

89. See the above poems by al-'Abbas ibn al-Ahnaf (750–809).

Scared he shut his eyes,
Watching the Yemenite lightning illumine the cup
Followed by drumbeats.
This is Baghdad, rising from one death to another, from
    her taverns
Gravediggers, vagabonds, and ghosts of thieves
All fall to the ground.
Pale, al-'Abbas follows suit,
Lighting the candle of longing,
Searching the cup for another girl.
Will there be any dance in this very long night?

Baghdad's taverns have darkened.
There is no use!
Al-'Abbas is dying of love.

(*1998*)

Shadhil Taqa (1929–74)

And When We Took Over Her

We have made Time white-haired,
But our desires have not been fulfilled,
And our hopes have not been complied with.
Many a war we fought for her . . .
And when we took over her
We gave her as a present to our enemies.

(Baghdad, 1964)

Adonis[90] (1930–)

Elegy for al-Hallaj

Your poisonous green quill,
Your quill, its veins swelled with flame,
With the rising star from Baghdad,
All are our history and prompt beginning,
In our land — in our recurring death.

Time laid itself on your hands.
The fire in your eyes
Swept away and spread to the sky.

Oh star rising from Baghdad,
Loaded with poetry and birth,
Oh poisonous green quill.

Nothing is left for those from afar,
With thirst, death, and ice,
In this land of rebirth —
Nothing is left but you and Presence.[91]
Oh Galilean language of thunder,
In this land of peels,
Oh poet of secrets and roots!

(1961)

---

90. A pen name of the Syro-Lebanese poet ‘Ali Ahmad Sa‘id Isbar.
91. The Presence of God.

Poetry Presses Her Lips to Baghdad's Breast
(Baghdad 1969)

[In 1969, I visited Baghdad as a member of the Lebanese
Association of Writers' delegation headed by Suhayl Idris.[92]
The aim was to participate in the conference of the Arab
Association of Writers. Nizar Qabbani was also in the Lebanese
delegation. I stayed there several days, without participating in
the conference's discussions for reasons I would prefer to keep
to myself. That has been my only visit to Baghdad. The
thoughts I now [2003 — R. S.] publish were written during that
visit, and I do it now, with some corrections, for the first time.
In order to refute interpretations which some people may
suggest, I would like to say that these thoughts are by no means
a judgment on the Iraqi people as a whole; rather, they are
based on impressions about the regime and its members and
the cultural and political 'atmosphere' that their supporters and
followers were constructing at the time.]

1

Light in Baghdad is less shiny today than yesterday when I
    arrived.
Can light get flabby, as well?
— Whisper, please! Every star here plans to kill its neighbor.
— Whisper? You mean as if I'm talking with death?

Men turn their faces toward shapes. Shapes without faces.
    Shapes like holes on the page of space.
Men walk in the streets as if digging them. It seems to me
    their steps have the forms of graves.

---

92. Suhayl Idris (1923–2008), a Lebanese writer, journalist, and publisher.

Politics have a wide market that all other markets envy.

Voices come from the theaters of the absolute:
The walls — even the walls yawn.

2

The political hammer knocks on the anvil of the neighbor-
hood where I stay. A celebration of voices — the
neighborhood comes to its ceremonies feeble, indiffer-
ent, lost in the dust of screams.

I say to myself: When will we know silence? I wonder, Will
paradise keep silent? Will hell keep silent? Is someone
brave enough to deliver a *fatwa*?[93]

I think the time has come to tell Gilgamesh.[94]
Gilgamesh! You have deluded some of us. You convinced
others that life in Baghdad has a secret that we are still
waiting to be revealed — mostly when almost every-
thing points out that life here is nothing but continu-
ous death. Please, look how the dictator's sword is
sharpened, how necks are prepared to be cut.

That very meeting:
— The issue concerns a small agent who was killed like a dog.
— How would the agent be killed if he were big?

---

93. *Fatwa* is a legal religious edict in Islam.

94. Gilgamesh, in Mesopotamian mythology, was two-thirds god and
one-third man. He built the city walls of Uruk to defend his people from
external threats.

Now, I understand how a bird could commit suicide,
   scared by a rifle that tracks it wherever it flies.

— Do you work? How do you live?
— I move from street to street. Baghdad is not devoid of
   beneficent people.

The head of this street is full of wisdom.

On her black wings a dove paints a circle around the
   Tigris's banks.

That very meeting:
People — each struggles to be the regime's parrot, the
   most eloquent of them all.

Baghdad: all of it is smoke, but where is the fire?

The more I penetrate into Baghdad's childhoods, the more
   I know about myself, about others and the universe, the
   more I despise her present.

"I do not have any relatives except the genealogy of the
   wind":
That's what an Iraqi man told me when he came to my
   hotel to meet me.

For the first time, I came to know that the left bank of the
   Tigris hates its right sister, and she hates it.

Now at this moment, it seems that I see in Baghdad two
   men:
Al-Hallaj[95] on the cross, and al-Tawhidi[96] tossing his
   books into the Tigris's waters.

Baghdad invents a special person for herself, a
   coffee-person.

Ishtar[97] is sick, al-Mutanabbi's[98] fever makes her tired.

The Tigris's waters nearly escape from both its banks.

Gilgamesh! Oh you, the first son, the first-born of the
   myth, will your poetry remain as a grounds for
   emigration?
Can it be that "no-return" is a homeland?
And as for friendship, who will sing of it after you?

Here, life loses its time waiting for death.

The engineering of men and women spreads the word of
   the windmills.

What has happened to Baghdad's sun? It rises each day
   with a blind child in its arms.

---

95. Al-Husayn ibn Mansur al-Hallaj (858–922), a poet-mystic.

96. Abu Hayyan al-Tawhidi (922–1023), an Arabic litterateur and philoso-
pher, probably of Persian origin.

97. The Assyrian and Babylonian goddess of fertility, war, and love.

98. Abu al-Tayyib al-Mutanabbi (915–56), one of the greatest medieval poets
in Arabic.

Freedom has only just one statute: Freedom.

I tend to believe that Abu Nuwas,[99] Abu Tammam,[100] and al-Niffari[101] did not live in Baghdad.

The demons in Baghdad, only they, are the hungry — wanderers, unemployed, prisoners . . . and so on.

Here, I am convinced that the dictator's mind is devoted to composing specific encyclopedias that hunt human beings and tame them.

River Tigris! I know full well that, if revolution were a ship, you would have been the first to destroy its sails.
In the past, pagans used to live on your banks, and yet they were more creative and human than their monotheistic grandchildren who besiege you today.

Today I got up as if I were a moon rising from the sun's body:
Right! She was the woman who put a rose on my room's window ledge; she came before the sun and returned to her home.

---

99. Abu Nuwas, al-Hasan ibn Hani al-Hakami (747–62–813–815), one of the greatest of classical Arabic poets.

100. Abu Tammam, Habib ibn Aws Al-Ta'I (803–45), an Abbasid era Arab poet and Muslim convert, born to Christian parents.

101. Muhammad ibn 'Abd al-Jabbar ibn al Hussayn al-Niffari (d. 965 or 976–77), a mystic and poet well known for his books *al-Mawaqif* and *al-Mukhatabat* (*The Stations* and *The Speeches*).

That very meeting:
Each speaker thinks he speaks the truth, uttering the last
   decisive word.
Each poet wants to be told: You are the first and the last!
Meerschaum clashes; one eats the other.

My friend J lives in what seems to be a palace. He told me:
   It is easier for this house to be destroyed than for me to
   open one of the windows you see before you.

How heavy is the day in Baghdad! Without her night, she
   would have been a prison.
With Nizar Qabbani. With you? Yes, we will come:
   Wherever and whenever you want.
She was speaking, strongly courageous. Her friend was
   listening, two gazelles swam in her eyes.
— And why this veil?
— It is the veil of the returning home. Especially at night.
   Tradition is a prison inside a prison.
— . . .
They disappeared, just as stars vanish.
The sun was rising on the Tigris's stairs.
The day was preparing to don its military uniform.
Night shot its arrow and struck.

Al-Karkh! I saw Sumar and Babel, they were like two
   wings — two threads between the sun's East and West.
   I saw something like a wave welcoming Ishtar when-
   ever she dipped her feet into the Tigris. I saw Ishtar
   herself, as if she were preparing for another love. At
   least, that's what it seemed to me.

3

The copper market![102] Young men and women! Their
bodies seemed to be a long history of night. During the
day, rust nearly clings to time's body.
Sewage systems, in open air, facing stores. Bad smells
plunder the empty space.

What am I listening to? Are they old houses' walls whis-
pering to me: Is there something other than memory
guarding me? Or do you think I'm only imagining?

Why don't I paint Baghdad's face on doubt's threshold?
The water of the Tigris cannot say no.
The necks of date palms cannot bow down any more than
they already do.
It's painting for its own sake, just for itself.

I have a quarrel with water that only remembers sources of
the blood that flows into it, water soaking in the
ferment of tears.
It is as if I see death waiting to hunt human beings.

At this very moment, I want to say: Baghdad! Half of her is
a forest, the other half a desert.
Oh my friend, I long to ask you in a whisper:
— What is the difference between Baghdad 1258[103] and
Baghdad 1969?[104]

---

102. *Suq al-Safafir*, the central market in Baghdad, which constantly teemed
with people and goods.

103. The year Hulagu destroyed Baghdad.

104. The year Adonis visited Baghdad.

The first, the Mongols destroyed; the second,
    her children do the same.

4

A café — coconuts like necklaces hung from trees that
    never grow, except in the earth of the imagination.

An old man breathes with lungs of childhood. Another
    one moans and stammers. As if he cannot describe the
    fire that flares up in his bowels. As if he does not know
    how to expel the sorrow that his father Adam caused
    him.
From the café, black smoke rises — is it the breath of
    people who lean on their coconuts? Is it a dream about
    another roof? Is it another land?
Through the smoke, sighs and mumbles rise, like floating
    bridges between events and memories, there is no
    clarity, there is no obscurity. Nets of letters where
    wings of doubts clash.
In each yes there is a no.
In each no there is a coal not knowing how to be
    extinguished.
Beneath the skin of this café, there are rippling oceans of
    refusal.

A bookstore! The writing of this author is curved, but his
    words are straight.
— This author is repetitive.
— Sometimes it is necessary to say the same in order to
    say something different.
— A poet like an angel.

— Is this praise or condemnation? The angel can do good and evil, but the devil can do nothing but evil. Who is more pure?
— This is an obscure poet.
— What is revealed quickly becomes banal just as quickly.
— Poetry? I do not know.
  Poetry is generous like the empty space, embracing even the birds that revolt against her.
— Here each person seems to be a date palm living on the edge of an unsteady cliff of sorrow, like the genealogy of Sheikh Ja'far.[105]
— Have you ever encountered people in need of oppression in order to feel that they exist?
— You mean the people of Iraq?
— But what can you say about a leader who climbs the plans he has placed on a mountain of human skulls?
— Tomorrow?
— Don't forget! Please whisper! Tomorrow is a restless bone in the wing of a bat.
— Please forgive his hallucinations.
— I am not a man of attachments or commitments. I can learn how to be a man of freedom. I can identify with an angry, disappointed, and nasty frame of mind. Exactly like you.
— Better to talk about women, about beauty. In Baghdad, there are women without whom time doesn't know how to get really drunk.

---

105. Ja'far ibn Muhammad al-Sadiq (702–65), a descendant of 'Ali whom the Shia regard as the first Imam and thus, along with his descendants, the rightful successor to the Prophet.

— And with women like them.
— I repeat: We should speak in a whisper.
— Men choke the air.

5

A woman embraces a window in a house on the Tigris's
    banks. An enlightened woman fears the light.
The Tigris is like a body dragged by a vehicle, dragged by
    fear.
The Tigris is the hymn of an encounter that is rarely heard
    by anyone.
— What is your profession? What do you invent?
— The threshold of the house has ears.
We have no need of thinking. There is someone else who
    makes it unnecessary. He knows everything and
    responds to everything.
Everything changes in the chemistry of politics:
Oh dove, what kind of a woman do you want to be?
Oh hoopoe, what kind of a man do you want to be?
Oh stone, which role do you want to play? And you, Oh lock?
An atmosphere that freezes words,
And the poison roars in the veins of the language.

Why does Baghdad have only one way,
When there are so many ways?

Baghdad seems to be a cage of words. As soon as a man
    leaves, the words open up and like barbaric jawbones
    shut down on him.

As if the mind were a rope around the neck.

Days become intoxicated in the face of red colors,
Without excluding the color of blood.

Time — like a body, the limbs swallowing each other up.

This is the sun that welters in blood on the streets.

Abu Hanifa, al-Shafi'i, Malik, Ibn Hanbal[106] — each one
    was granted an apartment in the skies, thus escaping this
    world. It has been related that each one dedicated his
    eternal stay in his own paradisical apartment to compos-
    ing books condemning the world and obeying its "rulers."
What is that sky-blue cloak that covers the Qadiri-
    Kaylani[107] holy presence in the mosque?

— Baghdad is a paradise?
— Man is a paradise, not the place.

— Do you want to stay here?
In that case, please lay down another navel in place of your
    own and replace your head.

Ether of tools fills the air.
In the science of form that this ether spreads, Baghdad is a
    mother with embryos tied to her pelvis. Each one
    emerges praying to the absolute ruler.

---

106. The founders of the four extant schools of Sunni Islamic jurisprudence:
Abu Hanifa (699–767), al-Shafi'i (767–820), Malik ibn Anas (711–95), and
Ibn Hanbal (780–855).

107. A famous mosque in Baghdad named after the Sufi master 'Abd
al-Qadir al-Kaylani (1077–1166).

And in the science of form, the absolute ruler sews the
    cloth which, for the first time, touches the skin of the
    embryo.
And in the science of form, Baghdad is a house of calam-
    ity's ants. As for myself, I rejected it all and withdrew.

Should I have accepted reality, spending my whole time
    only with what is probable?
Should I have declared publicly that every voice in Bagh-
    dad has a spur?

Ether of tools floods the air — penetrating all its parts, I
    hear those who used it to entertain vain hopes with
    time, empty space, the regime, corpses, and future.
This is how all aspects and horizons are arrayed in a new
    light.
From now on the land is an arrow whose bow is the ruler's
    throne.

Birds — wounds in trees. And this was a rose that was a
    string of perfume between the sun's east and west. A
    neck bows, eyelashes are broken.
No flash of lightning, only delusion.

There is a thirst enveloping the body like wrapping paper,
    and each minute seems like a bottle from which the
    bowels of history are spilled.

6

Leaning on the edge of the bed in a hotel (I have forgotten
    its name), I hear the chimes of an obscure clock, as if it

were hung from the neck of an almost dried-out date
palm. It is twelve o'clock, at night.

Night spends time by the Tigris. I imagine I hear
water coughing, banks weep. I address my warning
to you, Oh night, from within my darkness, and
you, Oh sleeping cities of the Euphrates, peace be
upon you.

On the tray of events, I throw my confused dice. I am
waiting, contemplating, discovering that events have
their winning dice.

What should I do? Should I surrender? Should I go on
pushing queries, like rocks nearly boomeranging to be
thrown at me?

And you, Oh my head, tell me: Why this storm in you that
refuses to be calmed?

7

Poetry presses her lips to Baghdad's breast . . . I left her,
while imagining that cities sometimes adopt the dream
of change, and take it into their houses in secret — as if
it were a secret lover. This reminds me: never before
had I seen words, as well, sitting around tables to eat, as
I noticed them in Baghdad. They swallowed up every-
thing: meat, oil, and bone, those who were born, those
who were dead, and those not born as yet.

And I saw how it happened that language was transformed
into a huge army of predatory beasts. Until that moment
in 1969, I had tried hard to distinguish between human
beings, demons, and gods, while watching "the men of
power in Iraq." Perhaps, that is why in Baghdad, when I

was in the arms of the sun, I didn't feel anything other
than absolute cold.
But I can still say:
Oh poetry, please press your lips to Baghdad's breast!

> (*Written in Beirut, 1969. First published in London, 2003.*)

Salute to Baghdad

1

Put your coffee aside and drink something else.
Listening to what the invaders are declaring:
"With the help of God,
We are conducting a preventive war,
Transporting the water of life
From the banks of the Hudson and Thames
To flow in the Tigris and Euphrates."

A war waged against water and trees, against birds and
children's faces.
From between their hands
A fire emerges in nails whose heads have been sharpened,
The hands of the machine pat their shoulders.

The air weeps
Borne upon a cane called earth,
Dirt turns red and black,
In tanks and mortar launchers,
In missiles — flying whales,
In a time improvised by shrapnel,
As volcanoes shoot out their liquid lava into space.

Move, Oh Baghdad, on your punctured waist.
The invaders were born in the lap of a wind that strides on
    four legs,
By the grace of their private sky,
Which prepares the world to be swallowed by
The whale of their sacred language.

It is true, as the invaders say,
As if that mother sky
Only eats her children.

Do we all too have to believe, Oh invaders,
That there are prophetic missiles bringing the invasion,
That civilization is only born from nuclear waste?
Old-new ashes under our feet:
Oh misguided feet, do you realize the abyss
Into which you have now descended?

Our death now resides in the watch's hands.
And our sorrows desire to fix their nails
In the bodies of stars.

Woe to that country to which we belong.
Its name is silence, and nothing is there except pains.
And here it is full of graves — frozen and moving.

Woe to that land to which we belong,
A land swimming in fires,
Its people like green firewood.

How glorious are you, Oh Sumerian stone.
Your heart still beats with Gilgamesh.

Behold he is getting ready to go down again,
Looking for life,
But his guide, this time, is nuclear dust.

We closed windows
After we had cleaned their glass with newspapers that
    report on the invasion,
After we had thrown our last roses on the graves.
Where are we going?
The road itself no longer believes our steps.

2

A homeland almost forgets its name.
Why?
A red flower teaches me how to sleep
In the laps of Damascus?
The fighter eats the bread of the song.
Don't ask, Oh poet, for nothing but disobedience
Will awake this land.

                                    (*March 31, 2003*)

[*Time Crushes into Baghdad's Body*]

What is this iron roof on Baghdad's shoulders?
The lips of the Tigris and Euphrates shiver; life is a jug
    about to break,
An idol of fat hugged by gaunt hands.
In each of its cells there is a lake of desire.
Desire's body rests on metal; her soul lies on straw.

How wondrous she is! A feather unshaken by wind.
Oh angel asleep beneath her navel, when will you arise?
Spring upward, Oh unseen waters!
You alone have defeated the desert.

Night almost scatters its stars on Baghdad's body.
Murmuring, sleeping, she waits for a prophet of wakefulness.
Laying her cheek on sand, she waits for a prophet of
    wakefulness.
She wishes the earth to be a book she could seal with her
    sighs while being possessed by a prophet of wakefulness.
Clay stands between her feet, splitting into many
    nations.
What happened to that tablet, the one that came down to
    her, full of life and its myths?
What happened to that tree which, it was said, the devil
    once ambushed as it bore fruit and still ambushes?
But, behold the river of history, how it flows into the
    language plain, emerging from Baghdad's wounds. A
    history that flies in my imagination as though it were a
    black crocodile.
Except for the stars, does anyone know where Baghdad is
    and where the Arabs are?
Behold! Here Time crushes into Baghdad's body. Her
    tears have no kin but exile.

Oh Baghdad, in order to know you, do we have
    to separate
Your names from their meanings?

(*May 10, 2005*)

Muhammad Jamil Shalash (1930–)

Baghdad and Dawn

From the depths of the greater people,
From the heart of the factory and threshing floor,
From our valley,
From our Tigris,
From our village, this green melody:
Don't be sad, our blood — Kawthar.[108]
Baghdad, may my blood be your ransom.
Don't be sad; dawn illumines with its face;
Baghdad is here; from our East it illumines,
A new birth of green love,
A birth of spring
For every fallen victim,
Baghdad is here, in our East,
Storming the splendor of a brown dawn.

Wahran[109] is shaken by melody,
The pyramid whispers to Damascus,
Palms in our valley
Speak softly to us,
Speak softly to Jordan River,
To Jerusalem, to the Holy Place,
And to the Nile, when will they act?

---

108. A river in paradise; the name literally means ample, abundant.
109. Wahran, Wehran, or Oran is a major city on the northwestern Mediterranean coast of Algeria.

Oh dawn of my tomorrow, treasure of my tomorrow,
I am still your brother; take my hand.
Take it, to support us.
Embrace our unity.
Use it to govern in our East.
Be generous throughout our homeland,
Throughout time, with a brown dawn.

The East arouses it like a dream.
The Nile blows it as lava
And consciousness as blood.
The East, and the brown forearm,
The factory and threshing floor,
And the shadows of date palm and cedar
Cry to us:
"Glory to us, pride to us,"
Palm and brown forearm,
In our East, in our West,
Still here, shout to us:
"With our fates, our disasters,
With our forearms, our victims,
With the blood of Kawthar,
Baghdad is here in our East
Storming the splendor of a brown dawn."

Baghdad will shine on our world.
Don't be sad for our victims,
Our disasters and fates
In all limbs
Of a morning's birth.
Baghdad, night will commit suicide;

Morning will rise
From a strong brown forearm
With green love.
Don't be sad; sighs never help;
Don't be sad; dawn will come tomorrow,
Baghdad tomorrow
With the moisture of Barada,[110]
The moisture of the Nile,
The moisture of the Tigris.
We will unite them as one.
We will shoot them as one,
And here will arise a brown dawn,
And here in our East it will stay.

(*June 14, 1958*)

---

110. The main river in Damascus.

Salah 'Abd al-Sabur (1931–81)

The Tatars Have Attacked

The Tatars have attacked,
Razing our deep-rooted city to the ground.
Our battalions return torn to pieces after sunrise,
The black flag, the wounded, a caravan of dead,
The hollow drum, unheeding, submissive steps,
Palms of a soldier playing on wood
To the tune of hunger.
Trumpets accelerate; out of breath
The earth burns, as if its fire were rotating.
The horizon is jammed with dust.
A destroyed vehicle rolls on the road,
The horses gloomily look on,
Noses bathed despondently,
Eyes of dispirited tears.
The ear is stung by dust.
Soldiers, hands lowered almost to their feet,
Shirts twisted, painted with tiny drops of blood.
Mothers had taken shelter behind the dark hill for fear of fire,
Or the horror of the rubble of destroyed buildings,
Or the contemptuous stare seen in faces of the Tatars,
Their hands extended in ugly greed.
Destruction and humiliation crawl forward
Oh my city! The Tatars have attacked.

In an isolated distant prison camp,
Night, barbed wire, and the heavily armed guard;

Monotonous darkness, the wounded, and the stench of pus,
Joking drunkards among the Tatars,
Licking their lips in victory,
Celebrating the joyous campaign.
But I have embraced my defeat and thrust my leg into the
    sand.
I remembered, Oh Mother, our long luxurious evenings.
My eyes full of tears, Oh Mother, I cried for a memory like
    a breeze and
Clouds of old words.
Oh Mother,
Among those taking shelter near the hill.
For children, night knits horror beneath eyebrows,
Hunger and thin garments,
Deaf people and female demons; darkness dwells inside
    caves.
Did you cry for our village because it turned into rubble?
Or because happy days of the past will never return?
Oh Mother, we shall never perish.
That is what I'd heard from folks in our ancient street,
A defeated cripple's cough,
And a mouth mumbling threats from afar.
And I — like all our friends — Oh Mother, when day fades,
We swear in hatred that tomorrow we will rejoice in the
    blood of the Tatars.
Oh Mother, please tell the children:
Dear children,
We will walk among our grey houses, when day rises,
And build again what the Tatars destroyed.

(1957)

Sa'di Yusuf (1934–)

The New Baghdad

She comes to me, when I am besieged by fumes of cheap
    arak,
With a bowl of soup.
She comes to me at dusty noon.
She comes to me each evening snatched by night.
With an evening star
In a café, she sits to quaff bitter tea.
In a market she sells cheese
And buffalo livers.
She dusts all her used-ironed-clothing stores,
Searching for bones in a bowl of soup,
For milk in a child's lips,
For a glimmer in a pair of eyes,
For something a woman does not know,
For streets where water never greens.

At night,
She roams among houses abandoned by the poor,
Among churches where a muffled mass fades,
And huts where poor girls faint.
At midnight,
She returns to her enchanted shelter, behind her muddy
    streets,
Carrying the bread of the dead,
Myrtle flowers,

Slivers of buffalo liver,
And two bones for a bowl of soup.

At dawn
She stops by all her houses,
Waking all her children,
Dragging them to the street,
Thousands waiting to march on Baghdad.

(April 8, 1975)

Solitude

One morning, I saw them hurrying by
Walking together,
Scent of almonds filling the street.
Are they sisters?
I noticed their somewhat practiced cat steps.
Why did I feel the scent of almonds follow me,
Something that I knew about two sisters
Walking in the morning hurriedly?
Every morning,
When the clock strikes ten, I worry:
Will they pass by?
They pass by.
I catch the scent of almonds.
I touch the soft side of a cat's paw.
They disappear among the trees,
Or around the bend,
Or by the ledge of my window's angle,
Sometimes they turn back.

I see a thread;
It connects my room
To everything.

(*January 15, 1975*)

Baghdad

My friend asks me: How do you see Baghdad?
The city is in accordance with her people, I say.
But, he said, they are you . . .
Therefore, I said, I will ask people other than them,
I mean, another Baghdad . . .

(*Amman, July 6, 1993*)

The Spoliation

American helicopters bomb the poor neighborhoods,
And mercenary newspapers in Baghdad
Tell indistinct readers about an earth that will turn into
    heaven.

That plague,
That monster filled with abscesses,
Rhinoceros steel,
Drinking a cup overflowing with blood from the bleeding
    people,
Arming himself with dead people,
Devoid of excuses,
The killer,

Standing in squares,
Inflicting damage on Baghdad, this night and that night,
No doubt, he will leave,
And then we will accompany him with lamps of spit.

American helicopters bomb the poor neighborhoods,
And mercenary newspapers
In Baghdad
Tell indistinct readers
About an earth that will turn into heaven.

(London, April 5, 2004)

Ahmad 'Abd al-Mu'ti Hijazi (1935–)

A Poem for Baghdad

In that case, our waiting in cafes,
Our vagabondage in airports at nights
Through the eyes of the passport checkers,
Through entertainment places,
Our meetings, a breeze from Damascus
And from southern Iraq, vestige of a sigh,
Our talks have never been lost,
Never been lost, my God.

I almost see you; you are on the bank of night,
Awaiting the explosion of tranquility
While you fix your gaze on the city's corners
Like sailors watching from the south of the gulf
Congratulating Baghdad from atop a ship;
As if shepherds from the north arrived in the
     springtime,
Reciting their poems for the sad country;
As if villages beset by floods,
Had moved their children into secured hills.

I almost see you
While you are at Caesar's gates,
Groups of poets, red foreheads,
Singing for love from dry lips,
Groups of poor people

Desiring the fortress of 'Abd al-Ilah,[111]
Groups from al-Aʿzamiyya[112]
Surging forward into the Tigris through the water,
Scared in case the dream should fall on dust
In the last battle, Oh God!

I am with you, my friends!
I am with you, raising memories as slogans,
Fighting in their shadows, singing for the day of
     encounter.

I sing for Baghdad; I smell her night.
I sing for the haven of peace.
I sing in her language,
As one of her sons.
I sing for the east wind.
I sing the *maqam*.[113]
I hang about with her Kurds; from them I learn their love
     for horses,
Their way of drawing the sword.
And I shout at night, *Viva peace!*

(*1965*)

---

111. Crown Prince Abd al-Ilah of Hejaz (1913–58) served as Regent for King
Faysal II from April 4, 1939, to May 2, 1953, when Faysal came of age.

112. A neighborhood in Baghdad.

113. The Iraqi *maqam*, a four-hundred-year-old genre of Arab music founded
in Iraq.

Sadiq al-Sa'igh (1938–)

This Is Baghdad . . . (Excerpts)

This city is amazing:
She was bombed,
Trampled underfoot,
Just as a broken watch is crushed,
But it is as if she
Were just born.
She is still heard ticking under the rubble,
Measuring her heartbeats,
Stroking her lost limbs.

An amazing city
In a state of dream and hallucination:
History remembers her poems by heart.
Her houses are devastated.
Her buildings deserted,
And yet her colorful flags
Submit themselves to April's caressing wind,
Rising on roofs and poles
Surrounded by worn-out rags,
Yet held taut by innocent aesthetic feelings
Without traversing the borders of pain and forgetfulness,
Waving beneath the sun and shining,
Coloring the faces of the poor and streets.

With the colors of skies and angels.
A city impaled by dreams of ancient times,

Her body inflamed,
Her temperature high.
In her depths reside
Anger,
Hunger,
And creaking teeth.

This is a city hunted by history,
By snipers, lovers, and poets,
By raiders, barbarians, and petrol thieves
Whenever it seems she is *kaput,*
A drawn-out shout
Resounds from the depths of her soul,
Floats on the air like a broken wave:
"To die or not to die,
To live or not to live,
To be or not to be,
That is the question."

Yesterday,
Schoolchildren rescued from a hellish bombardment
Left their classes for the neighboring lane.
They cheered another punitive bomb
Tearing the sky, like a flying saucer
Passing overhead beyond roofs and boards,
Beyond laundry-loaded ropes
To inflict yet more misery
On the neighbor's window.

———————————

As I have said, this city is amazing:

Snipers, prophets, and killers
Seek her out;
Angels, poets and holy men as well,
East and West,
North and South,
One of the world's beautiful cities,
Her depths are shaken by daily bombings
Without losing balance,
And, although her women
Whisper to their men at night
Lest the children should awake,
The men don't listen;
They continue to reproduce.

This city is amazing:
Her residents are always drunken.
Her stars are never sober.
She was bombed,
Trampled underfoot
Like a broken watch,
But she went on ticking,
As if she were just born,
From beneath the rubble broadcasting
On wings of broken light
A code for future generations.
Her heart keeps beating and beating,
With solidarity,
With the sign of the broadcasting signal,
With all the strength and determination,
In all the words that are left to it:

This is Baghdad,
This is Baghdad,
This is Baghdad.

(February 2007)

Samih al-Qasim (1939–)

Baghdad . . . (Excerpts)

The Mongols have unrestrained armies,
the Tatars' swords with no sheaths.

The rude infidels have mobs
that spread only corruption.

While you lie naked in prison, bleeding,
in chains, pale and weeping, bastards and scoundrels are
    cackling.

Baghdad, Oh Baghdad, my love kills me; when
will your love let me die and be buried?

In al-Kazimiyya[114] I have a sun I flirt with,
in al-Rusafa, a window for my poems.

Baghdad, Oh Baghdad, my fire is a thousand flames,
inside my body a heart that aches.

---

114. A northern neighborhood of Baghdad.

Should I seek protection from the map you have always
    been for me?
Should I renew my birth in the name of God?

You are not you, an Abbasid girl taken prisoner.
You are Baghdad, but where is my own Baghdad?

(February 2003)

Fadil al-'Azzawi (1940–)

Mr. Edward Luka's Profession

The legend is fabricated in the Book of Creation.
The tourist practices selling leather masks
While the one-eyed king on his collapsed balcony
Talks about the Hittites' invasion.

The act ends with Jean Genet laughing.
The institute students talk about a limping female
    director;
Rouge colors her cheeks; in her laugh the instruction
Embarrasses the janitors at the music department.
Mr. Edward Luka passes by
To al-Khallani bookstore,
But he fails in the recitation.

In Zeya Hotel, the orientalist forgets
His wife; he drinks apple wine at the bar.
Wearing a hat of feeble straw,
Summer oppresses Agatha Christie as she writes her
Detective novel about Babel.
In the third act of the comedy of errors
All heroes suffer, the thief dies.
Baghdad beggars learn to dance
At the Auberge nightclub.

Oh Judas Iscariot,
Give your face some meaning!

People fight one another before the altar
While from my doorstep I watch
Hunting falcons for embalming and
Think about killing someone still unborn.

The idea bothers the poet's mind with meters.
He goes to the market, bringing the promised golden
    scales,
Memorizing all Arabic meters, in the students' café,
Feeling ashamed of *fa'lun, maf'ulun, fa'lan*[115]
Picking up twisted voices
In the past's throat,
Writing two verses of poetry, lighting the abyss
Between present and future, inflaming his genie mule
With a whip and leaving like a lance,
While the love-game,
The poetry-lie,
The man-whore,
All are celebrating tonight at the International Club of
    Human Rights.

For the sake of poetry, he tears off the masks of reversed
    history;
For the sake of the word, you abridge the world.
I will rise in this exile
Outside marks of profession,
Lashing faces of poets.

                                                      (1965)

---

115. A representation of metrical feet in Arabic poetry. The third one is an
ironical fabrication by the poet.

In Baghdad's Night

In Baghdad, I see a thousand Jesuses.
Homosexuals stone him,
And he shouts,
Yet the wind doesn't hear.

(1965)

The Ten New Commandments

Don't light a match in a forest;
The bird fears the fire!

Don't sit when the sun rises;
Someone is looking for light!

Don't stop the wind in the desert;
It might bring rains to Bedouins!

Don't look in a mirror;
You might be someone else!

Don't spit in a bitter well;
When one day you are thirsty, you might have to drink
    from it!

Don't stay with a barren woman;
You might have a child with her by accident!

Don't raise your voice on a dark night;
Demons might hear you and, feeling lonely, come into
    your home!

Don't poke fun at a rope in front of a hangman;
He might execute you!

Don't keep your joys hidden behind a mask;
The wind might lift it while you're singing in the wind!

Don't embark on a history your hand didn't create;
You might fall under its wheels while it is moving!

(1974–75)

Forgotten Maps

In Baghdad, twenty years ago
I met an oddly behaved man,
He used to walk from one street to another,
With old maps in his hand,
Searching for hidden treasures
In ruins
Full of scorpions and vipers.

The man was not mad,
He used to bow before me whenever I met him on the
    road,
Offering to share with me
His treasure of which he had not even a penny as yet.
"Never lose hope, my friend!

All you need is
To dig deep in the earth."
That is what he used to say in order to encourage me.
But, in the end, the man died,
And I left the city in despair,
Forgetting to take his maps with me
Into exile.

(2002)

Sami Mahdi (1940–)

Ruins

There is nothing to prevent the sorrow:
Those houses were wiped out or almost.
Pride and might abandoned them.
Near their doors you may see children playing;
You may meet women quarreling,
But all that remains of the houses is here.
Their ghosts are fading,
Their looks withdrawn in silence.

You left them between two illusions
And took refuge in silence.

You never gave them any option but death,
And waited for them to die.

Here they are now, opening their windows.
— Did you see?
Here they close them in fear
And die.

(Baghdad, June 12, 1978)

May Muzaffar (1940–)

The City

Evening casts its anchor; there are no departing ships.
Winter's hand extends heedlessly
Pulling the warmth out of the city's heart.
From the houses' wounds flow their sighs.
Baghdad,
A pearl has settled on the bottom.
Is there a lover or magician
To steal into her ashes and
Bring it back?

(March 1991)

Mahmud Darwish (1941–2008)

Iraq's Night Is Long
To Sa'di Yusuf

Iraq, Oh Iraq — blood the sun cannot dry,
And the sun is God's widow over Iraq. The Iraqi
Murdered say to those standing on the bridge:
Look at me, I am still alive. They say: You are still the
Dead man searching for his grave in the spheres of the
    coup.

Iraq, Oh Iraq — and Iraq's night is long,
Dawn will rise only for the dead that pray half-a-prayer.
Never salute anyone . . . The Mongols
Come from the gate of the Caliph's palace on the river's
    shoulder
And the river flows to the south and bears our sleepless
Dead to the relatives of the date palms.

Iraq, Oh Iraq — graveyards are open like schools,
Open for all, be it Armenian, Turkmen or
Arab. We are equal in the lesson of the science of
Judgment Day. There should be a poet to wonder:
Baghdad — How many times have you deserted myths?
    How
Many times have you created idols for the morrow? How
    many times
Have you demanded to marry the impossible?

Iraq, Oh Iraq — here stand the prophets
Unable to utter the name of heaven. So, who is
Killing whom now in Iraq? The victims are shreds
On the roads and within the words. Their names are
Tufts of distorted letters of words, like their bodies. Here
Stand the prophets unable to utter the name of
Heaven, and the dead man.

Iraq, Oh Iraq — so who are you in the presence of suicide?
I am not me in Iraq. And you are not you. And
He is not but someone other than himself. God aban-
      doned the confused;
So who are we? Who are we? We are not other than news
In a poem. Iraq's night is long, so very long.

(2007)

Su'ad al-Sabah (1942–)

Hulagu

Oh Hulagu of the present time,
Remove from me the sword of oppression,
You are a melancholic person,
Tragic,
Aggressive.
You do not distinguish between my blood and
The points of ink.

(1999)

Below Zero

Oh Hulagu,
Don't be angry because of my words
If I reveal to you this secret:
I am in a state of boiling
And you are a man below zero . . .

(1999)

Sharif al-Rubay'i (1943–97)

Harun al-Rashid

Another cloud came,
Bowed and prayed for the caliphate's treasure
All of which was in your possession:
Space and voice and earth,
And glories of civilization.
Oh you, bearer of glory with your pleasures,
Leave us! Stick in the past's mud,
To be nourished by fairy tales.

(*Baghdad, 1967*)

Sargon Boulus (1944–2007)

In the Garden of Saʿdi Shirazi
(When He Was in Prison)[116]

The river flows, the guides out of sight in the forests. I am
   just a single day dragging behind him a resurrection of
   days. Wounded battalions smell the air that burns with
   dry blood inside the nose. Because the city of water is
   no longer remote. She is here.

Over there, a garden of roses and a golden cup of poison
   guarded by an angel with his very hands.

The river signals to me from afar, its eyes closed before a
   drunken mistress. Thus it stays until it reaches in its
   dream the river mouth.

But with my lips I inquire, better than a blind man, from
   wall to branch, from chain to horizons, the cry that cast
   light with its sword on kingdoms, that sign for which
   my chains bled.

(*1998*)

---

116. A medieval poet who wrote elegies on the destruction of Baghdad in
1258. See the poem of Saʿdi Shirazi.

Hulagu Praises Himself

I am Hulagu!
A sea of grass crossed by horses in silence,
Barges of fire knock on cities' night.
I am an idea in stone's mind,
Fate's tongue, and God's louse.
War is a virgin in a torn tent;
Silence is one of my enemies.
I am Hulagu!
A sea of grass
Crossed by horses in silence.
A sword hates having to wait in its sheath,
Beneath walls that dream of crows;
Walls, walls, refugees see me
In their dreams amid the ruins;
Prisoners sharpen a small straw from my horse.

(2003)

There

I find myself in that house
Managed by a woman I do not see the whole week.
She wanders aimlessly between the rivers. When she
    returns,
She ties her boat to my foot while I am asleep.
In deep silence
She drags her claw-scratched body to my bed.
Recently, freed animals in the alleys
Have started to be more fearless,

Attacking sick people and children.
There are news and rumors: It is said that
A great hunger, a plague, massacres . . .

And when dawn rises in its vehicles full of ammunition,
My neighbors knock their heads on gates
As a sign of obedience
Or unbearable pain.

(2003)

Hangman

Oh Hangman,
Please return to your small village!
Today, we have expelled you and cancelled your job.

(2003)

I Have Come to You from There[117]

The end of the year:
The year of the ends,
Weather and crows, tightness in my heart
Because of much smoking, some sickness
(Solitude,

---

117. Poet's note: "Yusuf in this poem is my old friend from Kirkuk, the Iraqi
writer and storyteller Yusuf al-Haydari [1934–93 — R. S.] who fell dead, from
hunger or despair or both of them, in al-Mutanabbi Street in the besieged
Baghdad. I heard about his death while I was in the German village of
Schöppingen where I was staying at the time in the year of 1997." (sic!—R.S.)

Anxiety,
Hidden pain)
Drove me away to walk all over this lifeless town,
To cut through this very corner
Where I met him face to face
Before night fell,
My friend,
The storyteller himself,
But something had robbed his eyes of light.
My old merry friend,
Himself,
But something had inverted his lineaments
From the inside; the eyebrows were white;
The teeth black.
When he smiled (not from joy), he seemed to be crying
From behind the sorrow,
As if in a undeveloped photograph,
As a burned picture
That would collapse with a puff of breath.
He met me when we emerged from a storm that
Started yesterday,
Hitting walls with signs of restaurants and stores,
Letting telegraph cables
Yell strongly in that empty square.
Yusuf, I cried, Yusuf!
What has happened to your face, Yusuf?
What have they done to your eyes, Yusuf?
By God, what have they done to your eyes?
Please don't ask, he replied.
It is destruction, he said.
I have come to you from there, he replied.

Not me, he said. No. Not me.
Not you as well.
No, not you.
They and the gods of the Zaqqum,[118]
They, and the owner of death standing in the door:
Refugees on the roads,
Children in coffins,
Women mourning in squares.
Your relatives are well,
They greet you from their graves.
Baghdad is a spike of grain to which the locusts have
    clung.
I have come to you from there.
It is destruction.
He said this to me,
Then walked away and disappeared,
Everywhere.

(2008)

Hulagu (New Series)

My horses are
Lighter than the wind.

Their hooves strike sparks
When entering cities.

---

118. A tree that Muslims believe grows in hell where the dwellers are
compelled to eat its bitter fruit in order to intensify their torment (based on
the Qur'an, al-Safat [The Rangers], 62–68).

War lies down as a
Submissive bride waiting for me.

Death speaks in my name
I am Hulagu:
A sword in its sheath, never resting.
Its shadow, wherever it throws itself
Begets a cloud of hungry eagles
Hovering over houses.

Where refugees
See me in their
Nightmares between the ruins.

And prisoners sharpen
A handful of straw from my horse.

(2008)

An Elegy for al-Sindibad Cinema[119]

There is a road
Decorated by ceilings the memory has washed
Till it became white, beneath a sky that reached the peak
    of its burning, where
I walk; my words want to ascend like castle's stairs
Like voices climbing a lost scale
A note after another

---

119. Al-Sindibad Cinema was established in 1952 at al-Saʿdun Street and was
closed following the American occupation.

In my friend's notebook, the *oud* player, my friend
Who died, because of his silence, in exile's loneliness.
I locate this voice, find the building
And open a door.
Our time, how it lost its tickets!
It runs in darkness like a small waterwheel,
Made voices of those who do not have a voice!
They told me . . .
That al-Sindibad Cinema had been destroyed!
What a pity!
Who will now sail on? Who will meet
The Old Man of the Sea?
Those evenings were destroyed . . .
Our white shirts, Baghdad summers,
*Spartacus, the Hunchback of Notre-Dame, Samson and
    Delilah,*
How will we dream about traveling to any island?
Al-Sindibad Cinema had been destroyed!
Heavy is the watered hair of the drowned person
Who returned to the party
After the lamps were turned off,
The chairs were piled up on the deserted beach,
And the Tigris's waves were tied by chains.

(2008)

Abdul Kader El Janabi (1944–)

One Day We Will Have a History

Those who move
Between the palms of names
Whose spiritual rays
Soured in the burn of cold,
Who have an eye open
To the dead of memories,
Sleep will control them.
They will dream of blue color
Splashed across the horizon of the hand
As though it were a sea
That the land plucked
From a far-off paradise.

(*1995*)

The Immigrants of the Interior[120]

What we want
Is not an elevator in the building of names,
A square for an unknown soldier,
Scissors waiting for a *qasida*
Rebelled against a rhyme
With no clothes.

---

120. Poet's note: "Written during the war against Iraq in 1992."

That man might depart and not return.
He might come in the dead of night.
He might rebel,
His eyes taking on
The serenity of alternative.

We want
A noon at midnight,
A moon in the sun's arms,
Rooms where the light of day
Never loses a child,
And a lump of that rival
To decorate the shiver
And the scar of fear.
What we really want
Is on earth.

Doubt and covenant,
Certificates we bear with us
To the hereafter
For the living.

Neither head,
Nor hand,
Not arm,
Not even that heritage.

Instead a wisp of history
In the blow of paper
Trimmed by a comb of difference.

(1995)

What a Moment Is That

When a people with no name —
Because it has no present —
Penetrates the anemones of explosion,
Chased by a past that has awakened
From a long nightmare,
Rolling its head at the feet of Mars
Arising from the garments of the North.

(1995)

Bildung

To G. E. von Grunebaum[121]

Here is my share of sand:
A purple soul
Born in a cosmopolis of the medieval world,[122]
They removed my foreskin;
They showed me my totemic ancestor,
Picturesque vestiges without redemption.
They taught me what guts are, what ink is,
Granted me the scripture,
Let me thieve through medieval nights,
Holding moon against sun,
Hitting on a solution.

---

121. This poem was written directly in English. The poet dedicated the poem to Gustave Edmund von Grunebaum (1909–72), a scholar of Near Eastern history, whose studies on Arab culture inspired him.

122. Poet's note: "I mean the city Baghdad."

When the day of reason broke,
They brought me a camel,
Sent me to work amidst the debris,
Splintering mirrors of otherness
In the hope of being attuned to that very rhetorization
Like a shadow moves back and forth
On the wall of creation.

They ordered me to heap
On the ground of knowing
References upon references,
To the point of making the perched birds of the brain
Fly from the skull of the book
Toward a groove
Open in their picture of the past.

And before falling asleep,
They advised me not to dream of perfection.
It's lagging behind,
They told me:
Decay is in the present.
Tomorrow is also decay.
Everything will fall apart . . .
Dust is master of all!

(Paris, 1986; rewritten in Paris, 2013)

In Baghdad, Where My Past Generation Would Be

To Jan Dammu (1942–2003), the only one who deserves the memory of bygone moments.[123]

Where are you, my first years,
Years of streets and cafés,
Years of days and long walks,
In the course of revolts with no pricking of conscience?
Where are you, my first years?
Oh my city, feverish with floods of memory,
Where are you in that drawn stream?
How can I write to you,
From the balcony to the water,
To restore to you seasons more remote than the two rivers,
To bookstores of boiling pavements,
To air-conditioned halls and concepts?
Oh my first years, years of a city
Where we used to drink the future in frightened gulps,
A city whose face is now polished with bullets.
With sunset the light used to come to her,
To spread above her roofs shadows and reflections.
The sky was shattered into stars to illumine darkness,
And from café to café,
We would search in the south of the known,
For the light of the north and write the hours
In antique notebooks of the invisible.

---

123. An Iraqi poet who was born in Kirkuk and moved to Baghdad to become among the "generation of the sixties." He emigrated to Australia, where he passed away.

We invented windows through which the other would
     penetrate beyond the fence.
We would long for their spaciousness and for a whiff of
     breath.
Where are they, my years spent strolling between days, the
     poets of temporal rest?
Who promised you the feat of dawn and mint
Whereas the well of their achievements
Is nothing but the verbosity of jammed sentences?
Oh God, if only they had been just once in the bed of the
     unknown,
Time would not have spared us a generation.
It would not have spared their odes the warmth of blood.
Oh years of white phantom,
Ghost of invented years,
The tide rises; the emotions augment.
Resistance is blind,
And you are immersed in thoughts.
What can I do with a memory
That cannot be but a memory?
What can I do with a past that is afraid of births,
Living only in the depths of those who have died,
Dying only in the clatter of those alive?

(*November 12, 2004*)

Faruq Juwayda (1945–)

Baghdad, Don't Be in Pain! (*Excerpts*)

Children in grieved Baghdad wonder
For what crime they are being killed; staggering on
    splinters of hunger,
They share death's bread, then they bid farewell.

God is greater than war's destruction, Oh Baghdad, and
    than loathsome unjust time;
God is greater than war's brokers acting against peoples,
    and than all traders in blood.

Baghdad, don't, please don't be in pain! Baghdad, you are
    flowing with my blood.
Baghdad, don't, please don't be in pain! Baghdad, you are
    flowing with my blood.

Baghdad . . . Baghdad . . . Baghdad

Oh! . . . Oh! . . . Oh! . . .
Oh! . . . Oh! . . . Oh! . . .

What a blot on the era of civilization!
How did threatening peoples become a slogan for fame
    and victory?
How did killing innocent peoples become a decoration of
    honor and pride?

God is greater than war's destruction, Oh Baghdad, and
    than loathsome unjust time
God is greater than war's brokers acting against peoples,
    and than all traders in blood.

Baghdad, don't, please don't be in pain! Baghdad, you are
    flowing with my blood.
Baghdad, don't, please don't be in pain! Baghdad, you are
    flowing with my blood.

Baghdad . . . Baghdad . . . Baghdad

Oh! . . . Oh! . . . Oh! . . .
Oh! . . . Oh! . . . Oh! . . .

Oh Baghdad, the object of love, my bitter wound!
Hurl your wounds onto my breast; hug my small heart.
Civilization won't survive without a heart or conscience.

God is greater than war's destruction, Oh Baghdad, and
    than loathsome unjust time.
God is greater than war's brokers acting against peoples,
    and than all traders in blood.
Baghdad, don't, please don't be in pain! Baghdad, you are
    flowing with my blood.
Baghdad, don't, please don't be in pain! Baghdad, you are
    flowing with my blood.

Baghdad . . . Baghdad . . . Baghdad

(2003)

'Ali Ja'far al-'Allaq (1945–)

Sketches in the Notebooks of Ibn Zurayq
al-Baghdadi[124]

The pillow of my face,
And a branch of water —
In its sleepiness, I bear your faces,
Oh tree of al-Karkh, and I forgot I have
Two years together with your life
Where I left my hands,
My wet age.
I came
With no eyes
From the dust of the salty tree.
I have a flower
That I bore from the firewood of poverty.
Didn't you see my hands as tatters
Full of wind?
My face a basket
From the spikes of the water wheel? These sad boats
a *qasida* the horses eat and resting upon it
As a pillow
Or a vehicle?

---

124. 'Ali ibn Zurayq Abu al-Hasan al-Baghdadi, a poet from the eleventh
century; see his poems earlier in this book.

Rawa[125]
Was a vessel in my blood,
From al-Kufa's rain;
Here,
In my hand the birds bowed, hanging their blue sleepiness
    in a kingdom.
I lost it on Monday morning,
And in the pale Sunday evening
The flower dried
On the edge of a rib.
The tribe of the eye
Cried.

The cold sticks
To the fingers of sleepers.
Which city's summer lingered
In my body?
Every wind in the ashes of the East
Is an amulet
Or a spike.
The western moon
Became a room,
Spreading on my face
The ink of moistened cities.

(*1973*)

---

125. A city that lies on the north bank of Euphrates.

'Abd al-Rahman Touhmazi (1946–)

What Do You Want?

I want!
I want!
I want air that will not mock my lung.
I want a spring that has yet to ripen.
I want a joint spring.
I want my heart's queen to thank my love. Oh!
I want sleeping people to take part in awaking me.
I want a spring that will not be ready for summer.
I want a spring that will collapse on me to make my nature
    pure.
I want blood that lacks no wound,
And wounds that blood never blinds.
I want!
I want!
I want a darkness that will be visible to me,
Lights that will not expose me.
I want a road to emigration that return will never take.
I want an *Iliad* that the *Odyssey* will never write.
I want poems that reject the shame of astonishment,
    consuming its meaning,
And other poems that do not perch in the shadow of
    words.
I want talk to guarantee my silence,
A peace where pity and excuses will be equal.
I want a question that will not adopt my answers,
A father who will not forget me,

A father whom I will forget.
I want!
I want!
I want a competition between freedom and sighs.
I want kings to celebrate the removal of crowns.
I want birds that will not deposit wings in a kernel of grain.
I want a tongue that the future will not embarrass.
I want a stone to be polished by the silence of wells.
I want roots laughing at the tyranny of branches.
I want howling to scare limbs of wolves.
I want high roofs in small cities.
I want thunder that is not polite to lightning,
And unhurried lightning in clouds.
I want!
I want!
I want ashes anticipating fire.
I want talking where voices are not connected.
I want a twisted time that attracts dreams.
I want Arab women
Who have great faith in love,
And men contained by some definition.
I want!
I want!

I want streets like ships,
And a space where my soul will remember my body.

(1995)

Bushra al-Bustani (1950–)

A Sorrowful Melody

The tanks of malice wander.
My wound
Is turned away like an abandoned horse
Scorched by an Arabian sun,
Chewed by worms.
Picasso paints another Guernica,
Painting Baghdad under the feet of boors.
Freedom is a lute
Strummed by a nameless dwarf.
Paintings in Baghdad's museums
Are at the mercy of the wind.
The Assyrian smiling bull is frightened.
Forced to leave, he is confused and weeping.
In the museum's corners and bends,
Sumerian harps
Played a sorrowful melody.

(2008)

Ronny Someck (1951–)

Baghdad, February 1991

Along these bombed-out streets my baby carriage was pushed.
Babylonian girls pinched my cheeks and waved palm fronds
Over my fine blond hair.
What's left from then became very black.
Like Baghdad and
Like the baby carriage we moved from the shelter
During the days of waiting for another war.
Oh Tigris, Oh Euphrates — pet snakes in the first map of
    my life,
How did you shed your skin and become vipers?

(1996)

The Shaving Razor That Cut the
Metaphor of Poetry
    To Abdul Kader El Janabi

He is the last hair in the curl of Salvador Dali's mustache.
He is the aimless shot in John Wayne's chopped-barrel
    Winchester.
He is the date that sweetened the paradise trees along the
    Euphrates and Tigris.
He is the shaving razor that cut the metaphor of poetry.
So, Abdul Kader El Janabi, what did we have? I asked,
On the sixth floor, in Rue Nollet, on the edge of the Clichy
    Quarter in Paris.

Whither gallop the horses of *One Thousand and One
  Nights?*
How much night was in one line?
How much love was in the eyes of his wife, Muna,
When his finger polished the picture's frame in which
He tried to long for his life's Western
In Baghdad streets?
In the other room, the freezer of consciousness was
  opened for a moment and
An ice cube sailed like a ship on the water that melted at
  the bottom of her body.

(1996)

A Personal Note on the Margin of a Renewal Form for an Iraqi Passport
  To Salah al-Hamdani[126]

Between the tailor's lips who will sew for me
The suit of return, a pin
Will shiver.
When he opens his mouth
The room will be pricked,
And the longing I invent for a treacherous Baghdad
Which has been erased from my memory,
Will be trapped in the tape-measure that is
Tied around his neck
Like a rope for hanging.

(2013)

---

126. An Iraqi poet (born 1951) living in France since 1975.

Wafa' 'Abd al-Razzaq (1952–)

The River

Weeping is sweet in the summer of the ferry.
He does not become tired from his sorrow on the street
    corner.
He leans on the back of the coastal road
And switches off his eyes in the middle of the road.
And in my white distress,
A loaf of bread is stretched out upon the dust of the voice,
And the last face of the river
Beseeches the soul
To paint the scattered fragments of my poetry.
But, since I left him,
He pronounces words imperfectly and utters my name in
    reverse.

(*2001*)

Ahlam Mustaghanimi (1953–)[127]

[Baghdad's Date Palms Apologize to You]

Baghdad's date palms apologize to you,
Oh you who departed early with time's birds.
This is not the time for you.
You have never been more full of life
Than when you were a guest in the cities of death.

Your steps embraced the pavements.
Your eyes were lips
Kissing children's cheeks.
You were desirable and waiting, like a prophet.
Therefore, you did not take care
When you crossed fate
To the other bank.

You wished then that your hand
Had been in the hand of the beloved.
You wished then that a last kiss had killed you
In an accident of love.
But you fell,
And the birds pecked up love wheat in your palm.
Perhaps you have gone to water with your blood
The tree of humanity.

---

127. Ahlam Mustaghanimi, an Algerian poet and novelist. The poem
appears at the end of her novel *al-Aswad Yaliqu Biki* (Black Suits You, 2012).

Oh lover who never returned from his dream,
Ignore death! Be strong!
Baghdad's date palms ask about you,
They ask me about you.
Perhaps the braids of waiting could provide consolation
And remove grief from young girls.

(Beirut, April 2012)

Ibrahim Zaydan (1960–) and Qays Majid al-Mawla (196?–)

A Joint Poem on the Live Half and the Dead Half

Mice,
They will come soon
Begging.
There is no waking,
But with mice,
Be careful
Not to be a mouse.
Should I be afraid of a trap,
Of hemp ropes,
Of shouts at night?
No, but you,
And no . . .
It bothered me
When I saw the people.
You were with me.
The mice will come.
The street before the mice.
It bothered me
When I saw caves
And women of clay
No . . .
But you.

The Plague
Creeps through my body.
Be careful.

Beware
A mouse might come,
Wishing to be your guest,
Trying to tempt your fear,
And finding refuge in it,
But in the end,
You will try to escape,
And you will be lost,
Even you.

Who whispered in my heart,
Expelled me, and threw me out?
Why?
I will not befriend the mouse
And teach it
How to be
And how to say
Who is mad.

Not the street,
Not the mice,
Not . . .
All of us,
We understand that the game
Is only hypocrisy
And a road that will please us
And be afraid
That it will lead to extinction.
Let us present our complaints
To a god
And a friend who

Lost his mind for love of mice.
Who has ignited that love?

Who divorced the woman of clay
And married her to water?
The mice gathered in the street
Bearing a sign,
Telling the unknown.
Therefore
I interpreted the things,
I came to you
With corrupted news
And words
Moistened with falseness.
I am imprisoned,
Anxiously I go
Wandering,
Looking for my other half,
For both halves to be with you.

We will hunt the mice,
We will dream of spoils
And cold rains.

(*Baghdad, July 7, 1985*)

‘Abid ‘Ali al-Rammahi (1967–)

Baghdad, Sing![128]

Baghdad, from hardship to hardship, sings,
Baghdad — my lover, my killer, my song, and my melody,
Baghdad, sing!
Oh a thousand of songs on a million mouths!
Baghdad — blood,
Baghdad — Mary shaking the stump of her date palm,
    dried out dates drop down,
Baghdad — spikenard overlaid with a wondrous gold bead,
Baghdad — Sindibad's boat wrecked on the rivers of the
    homeland,
And a thousand nights passed like strange clouds,
A female whose perfume the caliphs smelled,
And then the world disappeared, but she remained like a
    date palm at our home,
Baghdad — mother,
Baghdad — a minaret veiled in diverse tortures,
Baghdad — night engulfed by stars,
Enveloped by the fruits of the date palm,
Baghdad — a female bathing in the waters of the Tigris.
In silence she is lit with the silence of the lights of the
    glowing lanterns.

---

128. I thank Aviva Butt, who received the poem from the poet for her
screenplay *Love Under an Umbrella.*

Baghdad, sing!
Baghdad — my lover, my murderer, and my melody.

(2002)

Sinan Antoon (1967–)

A Letter to al-Mutanabbi (Street)[129]

How very right you were. Your words are still
Wings of light,
Always carrying you to us
(sometimes carrying us to you).
Your name is a green tattoo
On Baghdad's tired face.
Your street a forehead
On a head cut every morning.
This is another chapter
In the saga of blood and ink
You knew so well.
I cannot lie to you, Oh sir.
I'm quite pessimistic.
We are still here,
Engraving
On the walls of this cave,
Which is stretching to thousands of years long,
Signs we keep reinterpreting
And myths about a world
Where we don't devour one another,

---

129. The poet also wrote an English version of this poem that is slightly
different from the original. At the end of it, the poet added the following
comment: "Al-Mutanabbi Street in old Baghdad was the cultural heart of the
city, home to its book market and a café where the literati congregated every
Friday. On March 5th, 2007, a suicide bombing destroyed many of the
bookshops and killed twenty-six people."

Where the sun is friendly
And the seas don't complain from fever.
And . . .
Some of us are digging
A deeper grave
About to embrace us all.
They have nice engravings,
Maps, philosophers, and books.
But we can only keep
Dreaming of a shore for the wind,
And dig wells
In the dark
With nails of silence and solitude,
And weave an ocean out of ink
For our myths,
And out of words a sail
Or a shroud vast enough for us all.
Every book is a well
From which we drink
To your health,
Learning how to live
With death
And after it!

(New York, 2007)

The Milky Way

Your nipple
Is rounded years of strawberries
And my tongue,
A tribe of motherless fingers,
Reading the sleeping milk
On the dome of an atheist temple.
Angels and devils wail for asylum.
I swim in a fountain
Of undeciphered languages,
But they are the temporal way.
In the morning
Your bra strangles
My metaphors.

(2010)

Illumination

In the sky
The poles bow,
searching for what deserves illumination,
But the streets are overcrowded
With void.

(Baghdad, 1989)

Wars

Once upon a war
I took a quill
Immersed in death.
I drew a window
On the war's wall
And opened it,
Searching for tomorrow,
Or for a dove,
Or for nothing.
But I saw another war
And a mother weaving a shroud
For a dead man
Still in her womb.

(2010)

Dalya Riyad (1970–)

The Myth of the Tigris and Euphrates

At the dawn of the thirsty second,
The month of dates,
Year of eternal gregariousness and companionship AC and
     AH,[130]
The rain dropped in silence on the stairs,
Shaking its tail.
A mother in the courtyard of the house
Was repeating the call for the dawn prayer,
Baking bread, and
Wondering who sent the rain from the upper room.
The rain entered the room from the door ajar,
Looked at the angels while they were collecting their
     notebooks,
Pencils and musky erasers,
Then the rain mewed lazily and wondered,
Miaow . . . Miaow . . .
But Iraq did not move in its bed.
The rain leaped to a cup near the bed.
The handsome young man stretched out his hand
To massage the rain's back.
The cup fell on his hand and wounded it.
Two rivers flowed at once from between his fingers.

---

130. In Arabic the first three lines are formulated in the standard way of
denoting dates. I thank the poet for her assistance in the translation of these
three lines; I also thank Prof. Joseph Zeidan for his help in this regard.

One of them was mixed with his blood,
This was the Tigris;
The second was mixed with his soul.
That is how the Euphrates was born.

(2008)

Roadmap

If you were a microbe in my body,
Advancing from within to my skin,
You surely would pass Baghdad, in between myself and my
    skin.
And if you leave my skin,
You find yourself in Baghdad as well . . .
The map which terror could not change
Is Baghdad — my skin — Baghdad.
This is why, when I leave Baghdad, I seem like a skinned
    sheep,
And when I am inside her, I look like a sheep ready for
    skinning.

(2008)

Manal al-Shaykh (1971–)

Baghdad

There,
Where they gain a lot,
They have white towels sucking all desires of longing,
They have vehicles our disappointments drag,
Gilded by kingdoms' boys' breaths.
They pour in their silver cups
A little from our twilight,
And command a happy other person
To cut history's will
And avoid its last declaration:
There is no benefit from Shaharazad's tales
While women's silicone breasts
Are hung on new sultans' mouths!

(*2010*)

Afterword

Being a Baghdadi Poet: A Testimony

by Abdul Kader El Janabi

Poetry and Baghdad are indivisible, flowing together. One reflects then feeds the other, and so on. There is a relationship of city with logos, poetry with space, and it is no accident that Baghdad has produced hundreds of poets and few prose writers. The very essence of Baghdad speaks: its geographical position; the weather, too cold or too hot; Tigris River with its moonlit banks and dark floods breaking hearts into words; al-Rashid street with its metal balconies and stone columns stretched out for miles like Noah's ark preserving a cultural diversity; the old cafés and the markets of dawn; al-Safafir's copper shops (their prolonged hammering reminds you of how al-Khalil ibn Ahmad al-Farahidi invented the Arabic prosody); the vehement character of its residents and their openness to the new; the magnificent air-conditioned movie theaters (where you find yourself abruptly plunged from burning asphalt into biting snow); the bird catchers; the labyrinth alleys; al-Mutanabbi street — its bookshops bathing in a crowd of characters fleeing from all kinds of books; and the nights, long nights full of djinns and tales — rumor has it that Baghdadi poets prefer to write at night when their muses are at large. All this and more. The very nature of Baghdad strikes the match that ignites the poetic imagination of the Iraqis, and in a sense, of poets in the Arab world.

Baghdad is so rich with invisibilities that every poet has the possibility to bring a subject to light with no risk of duplication. His poem will certainly enrich the literature about this city, whose Persian-derived name etymologically means "the gift of God." Classical Arabic poetry always appreciated Baghdad's splendor and its being a city with the highest of cultural achievements. Even when poets glorified an ideal, Baghdad was the main subject matter — Baghdad, the city of dreams as opposed to other decadent cities. No other city so greatly aroused the interest of Arabic poets as did Baghdad, regardless of whether or not they lived in Baghdad or just read about it — the events of its past being always present in their poetic mind. Indeed, Baghdad is an easy metaphor for revival and eclipse — for what disintegrates into a lulling daylight!

In the aftermath of the Second World War and the modernization of Baghdad, Iraqi poets put forth new forms of poetic expression. The opportunity to explore "free verse" as a new diction prevailed alongside the newly born prose writing, such as the short story, literary criticism, and impressions. Subterranean Baghdad, with its informers, prostitutes, and beggars, loomed large in letter and spirit! Baghdad was no longer seen as a sort of shrine for pilgrimage, rather, for the first time, as a city gutted by alienation, antagonism, and poverty. It became a synonym for prostitution (see "Brothel" by Badr Shakir al-Sayyab)! Now it was thought that poetry should not praise what had already faded from the horizon. Poetry should call for social revolution, since it is the given moment that holds the microcosm of what flickers at each glance.

However, the poetic revolution with its new vision was set aside to await a new generation, the "generation of the sixties." The change could take place only when the city had undergone structural changes, and at that point would inevitably impose the structural change on the means of expression. A new atmosphere of "unexpected comradeship" prevailed, as ʿAbd al-Rahman Touhmazi correctly put it. As opposed to tribal membership, poets now felt that they belonged to a world-wide avant-garde. Baghdad figured as a metropolis, a state of mind, an explosive consonant, and was no longer mediated by nostalgia as in the classical poetry, or by militancy as in the "free verse." This is seen through the individualistic experience of the poet himself when he evokes images with contemporary Baghdad in mind. Poets no longer wrote poetry about Baghdad; they wrote poetry of Baghdad. In the first instance, poets tinkled their bells in order that nostalgia be remembered, while in the second instance, poets nibbled the sun's black teat in order to set the limpid substance of the city ablaze and wave to the magnet of time! Isn't it true that today Iraqi poetry seems almost to be a tour guide in the hands of readers seeking something new about this orphaned city? The new Baghdad was freed from the burden of past prestige and thrown into the turmoil of the moment. This gave poets an urban newness of seeing — the immediate experience of being a laboratory for experimentation in transmuting the ephemeral that modern life invariably spits out.

Baghdad, the city of cities, must be the only city in the world that can remain always the same whatever architectural clothes it wears. It is so very old — much as it is modern. This makes the poet feel as if he were in two different places at once: in a tent and in a skyscraper, in the real world and in a state of dream. The younger poets believe that their poems are nothing other than magic carpets to take them wherever they wish! — for the djinni is imprisoned in the word. You need only to break the syntax in order to unhook Baghdad from its old representations.

At the beginning of the 1920s, Baghdad became a capital of the united regions, communities, and formations called Iraq. Without Baghdad there could be no such Iraq. Every Iraqi has his own share of Baghdad, his share in its historical sufferings. It is only thus that he feels the poetic benediction.

I spent the best years of my youth in Baghdad. It was there, in that city, a city which is now falling into ruins, and stumbling through bullet and poem, I understood that to be a poet born in Baghdad means to be aware you are born in the middle of Mesopotamia. Its people are married to catastrophe, a destiny engraved on the tablets of myth, on the arc of the word: "When the God Enlil became restless at the noise of his people, and sleep wouldn't overtake him because of their racket, he decreed that half of the population should be done with!" The destructions of Baghdad perpetrated by Hulagu, Tamerlane (Timur-i Lang), and the last two recent wars are no other than a sign of the established alliance since the Flood. In every Iraqi poem, even the happiest one, there is *cette gravité*, that persisting sadness that is hidden behind an apparent seriousness —the solemnity of a city standing for centuries against history's barbarians.

> Therefore I consider the real Baghdadi poetry an act of
>   strategic hibernation
> Breaking through history,
> Escaping this given death,
> Bringing Eternity to Gilgamesh's knees,
> Installing within the Word a capacity for a true
>   endurance of the body and a generative adventure of
>   the mind,
> Keeping the trait of the human shape, and the principle
>   of hope warm and alive.
> It is the embodiment of personal courage to have a
>   universal outlook, to slash the veil between an
>   Orient of certitude and an occident of doubt.

Once, a friend asked me, "How can one become a Baghdadi poet?" I replied, "It is very difficult. It is like crossing a street without causing an accident! Or like being a madman with a flower in his hand trying to stab his own silhouette with it!"

REFERENCES
INDEX OF POETS
INDEX OF TITLES

References

Abbott, Nabia. *Two Queens of Baghdad: Mother and Wife of Harun al-Rashid*. Chicago: University of Chicago Press, 1946.

'Abd al-Rahim, Ra'id Mustafa Hasan. *Fann al-Ritha' fi al-Shi'r al-'Arabi fi al-'Asr al-Mamaluki al-Awwal*. Amman: Dar al-Razi, 2003.

'Abd al-Razzaq, Wafa'. *Li-l-Maraya Shams Mablulat al-Ahdab*. Irbid: Dar al-Kindi li-l-Nashr wa-l-Tawzi', 2001.

'Abd al-Sabur, Salah. *Diwan*. Beirut: Dar al-'Awda, 1972.

Abu-Lughod, Ibrahim. *Arab Rediscovery of Europe: A Study in Cultural Encounters*. Princeton: Princeton University Press, 1963.

Abu-Lughod, Janet L. "The Islamic City — Historic Myth, Islamic Essence, and Contemporary Relevance." *International Journal of Middle East Studies* 19 (1987): 155–76.

Abu al-Mutahhar al-Azdi, Muhammad ibn Ahmad. *Hikayat Abi al-Qasim al-Baghdadi*. Edited by Adam Mez. Heidelberg: Carl Winters Universitätsbuchhandlung, 1902.

Abu Nuwas. *Diwan*. Beirut: Dar al-Kitab, 1984.

Addas, Claude. *Quest for the Red Sulphur: The Life of Ibn Arabi*. Translated by Peter Kingsley. Cambridge: Islamic Texts Society, 1993.

Adunis. *Aghani Mihyar al-Dimashqi*. Beirut: Dar al-'Awda, 1961.

———. *Ra's al-Lugha Jism al-Sahra'*. Beirut: Dar al-Saqi, 2008.

———. *Warraq Yabi' Kutub al-Nujum*. Beirut: Dar al-Saqi, 2008.

al-'Afif, Ahmad Khulayf. *al-Tatawwur al-Idari li-l-Dawla al-'Iraqiyya fi al-Intidab al-Baritani (1922–1932)*. Amman: Dar Jarir li-l-Nashr wa-l-Tawzi', 2008.

Ali, Samer M. *Arabic Literary Salons in the Islamic Middle Ages: Poetry, Public Performance and the Presentation of the Past*. Notre Dame, IN: University of Notre Dame Press, 2010.

al-'Allaq, 'Ali Ja'far. *al-A'mal al-Shi'riyya*. Beirut: al-Mu'assasa al-'Arabiyya li-l-Dirasat wa-l-Nashr, 2008.

Altoma, Salih J. "Lami'ah Abbas Amarah: Elegiac Reflections on the 1991 Gulf War." *International Journal of Contemporary Iraqi Studies* 1, no. 3 (2007): 421–30.

315

al-Alusi, Jamal al-Din. *Baghdad fi al-Shi'r al-'Arabi min Ta'rikhiha wa-Akhbariha al-Hadariyya*. Baghdad: Matba'at al-Majma' al-'Imi al-'Iraqi, 1987.

Antoon, Sinan. *The Baghdad Blues*. Brownsville, VT: Harbor Mountain Press, 2007.

Antun, Sinan. *Layl Wahid fi Kull al-Mudun*. Cologne: Al-Kamel Verlag, 2010.

Arberry, Arthur J. *The Koran Interpreted*. Oxford: Oxford University Press, 1979 [1964].

'Awwad, Mikha'il. *Hadarat Baghdad fi al-'Asr al-'Abbasi*. Beirut: al-Dar al-'Arabiyya li-l-Mawsu'at, 2010.

al-'Azzawi, Fadil. *al-Ruh al-Hayya: Jil al-Sittinat fi al-'Iraq*. Damascus: Dar al-Mada, 1997.

———. *al-A'mal al-Shi'riyya*. Cologne: Al-Kamel Verlag, 2007.

Baghdad fi al-Shi'r al-'Arabi (Ja'izat Sha'ir Makka Muhammad Hasan Faqi, Ihtifaliyyat al-Dawra al-Tasi'a). Riyadh: Mu'assasat Yamani al-Thaqafiyya al-Khayriyya, 2008.

Bashkin, Orit. *The Other Iraq: Pluralism and Culture in Hashemite Iraq*. Stanford: Stanford University Press, 2009.

Basri, Mir. *Aghani al-Hubb wa-l-Khulud*. Jerusalem: Rabitat al-Jami'iyyin al-Yahud al-Nazihim min al-'Iraq, 1991.

Batatu, Hanna. *The Old Social Classes and the Revolutionary Movements of Iraq*. Princeton: Princeton University Press, 1978.

al-Bayyati, 'Abd al-Wahhab. *Diwan*. Beirut: Dar al-'Awda, 1972.

———. *Bustan 'A'isha*. Cairo and Beirut: Dar al-Shuruq, 1989.

Bell, Daniel A., and Avner de-Shalit. *The Spirit of Cities: Why the Identity of a City Matters in a Global Age*. Princeton: Princeton University Press, 2011.

Bell, Gertrude Lowthian. *The Letters of Gertrude Bell*. Edited by Lady Bell. Harmondsworth, UK: Penguin Books, 1939.

Benjamin II, Rabbi Israel-Joseph. *Cinq Années de Voyage en Orient, 1846–1851*. Paris: Michel Levy Frères, 1856.

Bosworth, C. E. *The Islamic Dynasties*. Edinburgh: Edinburgh University Press, 1967.

Boyle, J. A. ed. *The Cambridge History of Iran*, V. Cambridge: Cambridge University Press, 1968.

Browne, Edward G. *A Literary History of Persia*. Cambridge: Cambridge University Press, 1951.

al-Buhturi, Abu 'Ubada. *Diwan*. Beirut: Dar al-Kitab al-'Arabi, 2004.

Bulus, Sarkun. *Idha Kuntu Na'iman fi Markab Nuh*. Cologne: Al-Kamel Verlag, 1998.

———. *al-Wusul ila Madinat Ayna*. Cologne: Al-Kamel Verlag, 2003.

———. *'Azama Ukhra l-Kalb al-Qabila*. Cologne: Al-Kamel Verlag, 2008.

al-Bustani, Bushra. *Contemporary Poetry from Iraq*. Lewiston, NY: Edwin Mellen Press, 2008.

al-Bustani, Butrus. *Khutba fi Adab al-'Arab*. Beirut: al-Matba'a al-Amirkaniyya, 1859.

Carter, B. L. *The Copts in the Egyptian Politics*. London: Croom Helm, 1986.

Casey, Robert Joseph. *Baghdad and Points East*. New York: McBride, 1931.

Cleveland, William L. *The Making of an Arab Nationalist: Ottomanism and Arabism in the Life and Thought of Sati' al-Husri*. Princeton: Princeton University Press, 1971.

Cohen, Hayyim J. *The Jews of the Middle East 1860–1972*. Jerusalem: Israel Universities Press, 1973.

Coke, Richard. *Baghdad: The City of Peace*. London: T. Butterworth, 1935 [1927].

De Somogyi, Joseph. "A *Qasida* on the Destruction of Baghdad by the Mongols." *Bulletin of the School of Oriental and African Studies* 7 (1933): 41–48.

De Gaury, Gerald. *Three Kings in Baghdad, 1921–1958*. London: Hutchinson, 1961.

al-Dhahabi, Muhammad ibn Ahmad. *Ta'rikh al-Islam wa-Wafayat al-Mashahir wa-l-A'lam*. Beirut: Dar al-Kitab al-'Arabi, 1988–2004.

D'Ohsson, C. *Histoire des Mongols depuis Tchinguiz-Khan jusqu'a Timour Bey ou Tamerlan*. The Hague and Amsterdam: Les Frères van Cleef, 1834–35.

Dougherty, James. *The Fivesquare City: The City in the Religious Imagination.* Notre Dame, IN: University of Notre Dame Press, 1980.

Duclos, Diane. "Cosmopolitanism and Iraqi Migration: Artists and Intellectuals from the 'Sixties and Seventies Generations' in Exile." In *Writing the Modern History of Iraq: Historiographical and Political Challenges,* edited by Jordi Tejel, Peter Sluglett, Riccardo Bocco, and Hamit Bozarslan, 391–401. Singapore: World Scientific Publishing, 2012.

Duri, Abdel 'Aziz. "Governmental Institutions." In *The Islamic City (Selected Papers from the Colloquium Held at the Middle East Centre, Faculty of Oriental Studies, Cambridge, United Kingdom, from 19 to 23 July 1976),* edited by R. B. Serjeant, 52–65. Paris: Unesco, 1980.

———. "Baghdad." *Encyclopaedia of Islam, Second Edition.* BrillOnline, 2012.

al-Duri, Khidr J. *Society and Economy of Iraq under the Seljuqs (1055–1160 A.D.) with Special Reference to Baghdad.* Ann Arbor, MI: University Microfilms International, 1985.

Eco, Umberto. *Il Nome Della Rosa.* Milan: Gruppo Editoriale Fabbri, 1980.

———. *The Name of the Rose.* Translated by W. Weaver. London: Picador, 1984.

Eickelman, Dale. "Is There an Islamic City?" *International Journal of Middle Eastern Studies* 5 (1974): 274–94.

El-Ali, Saleh Ahmad. "The Foundation of Baghdad." In *The Islamic City: A Colloquium (Held at all Souls College, June 28–July 2, 1965),* edited by A. H. Hourani and S. M. Stern, 87–101. Oxford: Bruno Cassirer; Philadelphia: University of Pennsylvania Press, 1970.

El Janabi, Abdul Kader. *Stance in the Desert: Surrealist Writings (1974–1986).* Paris: Gilgamesh Publication, 1996.

Geary, Grattan. *Through Asiatic Turkey: Narrative of a Journey from Bombay to the Bosphorous.* London: Sampson Low, Marston, Searle, & Rivington, 1878.

Gibb, H. A. R. *Arabic Literature.* Oxford: Oxford University Press, 1963.

Goldziher, I. *A Short History of Classical Arabic Literature.*
Hildesheim: Georg Olms, 1966.

Gorton, T. J. *Voices of Arabia: A Collection of the Poetry of Place.*
London: Eland, 2009.

Haddad, Mishil. *Fi al-Nahiya al-Ukhra.* Shfram: Dar al-Mashriq,
1985.

al-Hajj, 'Aziz. *Baghdad Dhalika al-Zaman.* Beirut: al-Mu'assasa
al-'Arabiyya li-l-Dirasat wa-l-Nashr, 1999.

al-Hallaj, al-Husayn ibn Mansur. *Diwan al-Hallaj.* Edited by 'Abduh
Wazin. Beirut: Dar al-Jadid, 1998.

al-Hamadhani, Abu al-Fadl. *The Maqamat of Badi' al-Zaman
al-Hamadhani.* Translated by W. J. Prendergast. London: Curzon
Press, 1973.

al-Hamadhani, Badi al-Zaman. *Maqamat Abi al-Fadl Badi' al-Zaman
al-Hamadhani.* Beirut: al-Dar al-Muttahida li-l-Nashr, 1983.

Hämeen-Anttila, Jaakko. *Maqama: A History of a Genre.* Wiesbaden:
Harrassowitz, 2002.

———. "Building an Identity: Place as an Image of Self in Classical
Arabic Literature." *QSA* 3 (2008): 25–38.

al-Hariri, Abu Muhammad. *The Assemblies of al-Hariri.* Translated by
Thomas Chenery. Farnborough, UK: Gregg, 1969 [1867].

———. *The Assemblies of al-Hariri: Fifty Encounters with the Shaykh
Abu Zayd of Seruj.* Retold by Amina Shah from the Makamat of
al-Hariri of Basra. London: Octagon Press, 1980.

———. *Maqamat al-Hariri.* Beirut: Dar Beirut, 1985.

Hartigan, Karelisa. *The Poets and the Cities: Selections from the
Anthology about Greek Cities.* Meisenheim am Glan: Hain, 1979.

al-Hassun, Khalil Bunyan. *Ashja' al-Sulami, Hayatuhu wa-Shi'ruhu.*
Beirut: Dar al-Masira, 1981.

al-Haydari, Buland. *Diwan.* Beirut: Dar al-'Awda, 1980.

———. *Abwab ila al-Bayt al-Dayyiq.* London: Riyad al-Rayyis, 1990.

———. *al-A'mal al-Kamila.* Kuwait: Dar Su'ad al-Sabah, 1993.

Hijazi, Ahmad 'Abd al-Mu'ti. *Diwan.* Beirut: Dar al-'Awda, 1982.

Hinske, Norbert, ed. *Was ist Aufklärung? Beiträge aus der Berlinischen Monatsschrift*. Darmstadt: Wissenschaftliche Buchgesellschaft, 1973.

Hitti, P. K. *History of the Arabs*. London: Macmillan, 1946.

Hottinger, Arnold. "Patriotismus und Nationalismus bei den Araben." *Neue Zürcher Zeitung*, May 12, 1957.

Hourani, A. H., and S. M. Stern, eds. *The Islamic City: A Colloquium (Held at all Souls College, June 28–July 2, 1965)*. Oxford: Bruno Cassirer; Philadelphia: University of Pennsylvania Press, 1970.

al-Husni, 'Abd al-Razzaq. *Ta'rikh al-Hukumat al-'Iraqiyya*. Beirut: Matba'at Dar al-Kutub, 1974.

al-Husri, Abu Khaldun Sati'. *al-'Uruba Awwalan!* Beirut: Dar al-'Ilm li-l-Malayin, 1965 [1955].

Ibn al-Ahnaf, al-'Abbas. *Diwan*. Edited by Majid Tarrad. Beirut: Dar al-Kitab al-'Arabi, 1993.

Ibn al-'Arabi, Muhyi al-Din. *Tarjuman al-Ashwaq*. Beirut: Dar Sadir, 1966.

———. *Tarjuman al-Ashwaq*. Translated by R. A. Nicholsen. London: Theosophical Publishing House, 1978.

Ibn al-Dahhak, al-Husayn. *Diwan*. Edited by Jalil al-'Atiyya. Cologne: Al-Kamel Verlag, 2005.

Ibn al-Fuwati, 'Abd al-Razzq ibn Ahmad. *al-Hawadith al-Jami'a wa-l-Tajarib al-Naif'a fi al-Mi'a al-Sabi'a*. Beirut: Dar al-Kutub al-'Ilmiyya, 2003.

———. *Manaqib Baghdad*. Amman: Dar al-Faruq, 2008.

Ibn al-Hajjaj. *Taltif al-Mizaj min Shi'r Ibn al-Hajjaj*. Susa, Tunis: Dar al-Ma'arif li-l-Tiba'a wa-l-Nashr, 2001.

Ibn al-Jahm, 'Ali. *Diwan*. Edited by Khalil Mardam. Beirut: Dar al-Afaq al-Jadida, 1981.

Ibn Munqidh, Usama. *al-Badi' fi Naqd al-Shi'r*. Edited by Ahmad Ahmad Badawi and Hamid 'Abd al-Majid. Cairo: Mustafa al-Babai al-Halabi, 1960.

———. *Diwan*. Edited by Ahmad Ahmad Badawi and Hamid 'Abd al-Majid. Beirut: 'Alam al-Kitab, 1983.

Ibn al-Mu'tazz, 'Abd Allah. *Diwan*. Edited by Yusuf Shukri Farahat. Beirut: Dar al-Jil, 1995.

Ibn Qutayba, 'Abd Allah ibn Muslim. *'Uyun al-Akhbar*. Cairo: Matba'at Dar al-Kutub al-Misriyya, 1928.

Ibn Rashiq al-Qayrawani. *al-'Umda*. Edited by Muhammad Muhyi al-Din 'Abd al-Hamid. Cairo: al-Maktaba al-Tijariyya al-Kubra, 1963.

Ibn al-Rumi. *Diwan*. Beirut: Dar al-Kutub al-'Ilmiyya, 1994.

Ibn Taghribirdi, Jamal al-Din. *al-Nujum al-Zahira fi Muluk Misr wa-l-Qahira*. Cairo: Matba'at Dar al-Kutub, 1992.

al-Isfahani, Abu al-Faraj. *Kitab al-Aghani*. Beirut: Dar Ihya' al-Turath al-Islami, 1997.

al-Jahiz, Abu al-'Uthman. *Kitab al-Hayawan*. Edited by Muhammad Harun 'Abd al-Salam. Cairo: Mustafa al-Babi al-Halbi, 1938.

al-Janabi, 'Abd al-Qadir, ed. *Infiradat al-Shi'r al-'Iraqi al-Jadid*. Cologne: Al-Kamel Verlag, 1993.

———. *Hayat Ma Ba'da al-Ya'*. Paris: Manshurat Faradis, 1995.

———. *Inhatni fi al-Daw' li-Kay la Tusab Lughati bi-l-Duwar*. Beirut: Dar al-Ghawun, 2012.

al-Jawari, Ahmad 'Abd al-Sattar. *al-Shi'r fi Baghdad hatta Nihayat al-Qarn al-Thalith al-Hijri*. Beirut: al-Mu'assasa al-'Arabiyya li-l-Dirasat wa-l-Nashr, 2006.

Jayyusi, Salma K., Renata Holod, Attilio Petruccioli, and André Raymond, eds. *The City in the Islamic World*. Leiden: Brill, 2008.

al-Jazrawi, Ahmad. *Baghdad ba'd al-Gharib wa-l-Tarif min Madiha al-Zarif*. Baghdad: Dar al-Shu'un al-Thaqafiyya al-'Amma, 2005.

al-Jizani, Zahir, and Salam Kazim. *al-Mawja al-Jadida: Namadhij min al-Shi'r al-'Iraqi al-Hadith 1975–1986*. Baghdad: Dar al-Shu'un al-Thaqafiyya al-'Amma, 1986.

Johnston, John H. *The Poet and the City: A Study in Urban Perspectives*. Athens: University of Georgia Press, 1984.

Kant, Immanuel. "An Answer to the Question: What Is Enlightenment?" Translated by James Schmidt. In *What Is Enlightenment?*

Eighteenth-Century Answers and Twentieth-Century Questions, edited by James Schmidt, 58–64. Berkeley: University of California Press, 1996.

Kedourie, Elie. "The Break between Muslims and Jews in Iraq." In *Jews among Arabs: Contacts and Boundaries,* edited by Mark R. Cohen and Abraham L. Udovitch, 21–63. Princeton: The Darwin Press, 1989.

Kennedy, Hugh. *When Baghdad Ruled the Muslim World: The Rise and Fall of Islam's Greatest Dynasty.* Cambridge, MA: Da Capo Press, 2005.

Khalis, Walid Mahmud. *Baghdad al-Ta'rikh wa-l-Shi'r.* Beirut: al-Mu'assasa al-'Arabiyya li-l-Dirasat wa-l-Nashr, 2005.

Khan, Hasan-Uddin. "Identity, Globlization, and the Contemporary Islamic City." In *The City in the Islamic World*, edited by Salma K. Jayyusi, Renata Holod, Attilio Petruccioli, and André Raymond, 1035–62. Leiden: Brill, 2008.

al-Khatib al-Baghdadi, Abu Bakr Ahmad ibn 'Ali. *Ta'rikh Baghdad.* Baghdad: Matba'at al-Sa'ada, 1931.

Kiyotaki, Keiko. "Ottoman Land Policies in the Province of Baghdad, 1831–1881." Ph.D. diss., The University of Wisconsin, 1997.

al-Kutubi, Ibn Shakir. *Fawat al-Wafayat wa-l-Dhayl 'alayha.* Beirut: Dar Sadir, 1974.

Lapidus, Ira M. *Middle Eastern Cities.* Berkeley: University of California Press, 1969.

———. *A History of Islamic Societies.* Cambridge: Cambridge University Press, 2002.

Lassner, Jacob. "The Caliph's Personal Domain: The City Plan of Baghdad Re-Examined." In *The Islamic City: A Colloquium (Held at All Souls College, June 28–July 2, 1965)*, edited by A. H. Hourani and S. M. Stern, 103–18. Oxford: Bruno Cassirer; Philadelphia: University of Pennsylvania Press, 1970.

———. *The Topography of Baghdad in the Early Middle Ages: Text and Studies.* Detroit, MI: Wayne State University Press, 1970.

Le Strange, Guy. *Baghdad during the Abbasid Caliphate: From Contemporary Arabic and Persian Sources.* Oxford: Clarendon Press, 1900.

Levy, Reuben. *A Baghdad Chronicle.* Philadelphia: Porcupine Press, 1977 [1929].

Lewis, Bernard. *The Middle East and the West.* London: Weidenfeld and Nicolson, 1968.

———. *Islam in History: Ideas, Men and Events in the Middle East.* London: Alcove Press, 1973.

Longrigg, Stephen Hemsley, *Four Centuries of Modern Iraq.* Oxford: Clarendon Press, 1925.

Longrigg, Stephen Hemsley, and Frank Stoakes. *Iraq.* New York: Fredrick A. Praeger, 1958.

Lyall, Charles James, ed. *Translation of Ancient Arabian Poetry.* London: Williams & Norgate, 1930.

MacDonnell, Joseph F. *Jesuits by the Tigris: Men for Others in Baghdad.* Boston: Jesuit Mission Press, 1994.

Mahdi, Sami. *al-A'mal al-Shi'riyya 1965–1985.* Baghdad: Dar al-Shu'un al-Thaqafiyya al-'Amma, 1986.

Makiya, Kanan. *The Monument: Art and Vulgarity in Saddam Hussein's Iraq.* London: I. B. Tauris, 2004.

Al-Mala'ika, Nazik. *Diwan.* Beirut: Dar al-'Awda, 1979.

Malitan, 'Abd Allah Salim, ed. *Baghdad, al-Shawq wa-l-Hisar: al-'Iraq fi al-Shi'r al-Libi.* Tripoli, Libya: Dar Midad li-l-Tiba'a wa-l-Nashr, 2007.

Marun, Jurj Khalil. *Shu'ara' al-Amkina wa-Ash'aruhum fi Mu'jam al-Buldan li-Yaqut al-Hamawi.* Beirut: al-Maktaba al-'Asriyya, 1997.

al-Mashhadani, Mahmud. *Baghdad fi 'Uyun al-Shu'ara'.* Damascus: Dar Ninawa, 2009.

Matlub, Ahmad. *al-Madina fi al-Turath.* Baghdad: Matba'at al-Majma' al-'Ilmi al-'Iraqi, 1994.

Micheau, Françoise. "Baghdad in the Abbasid Era: A Cosmopolitan and Multi-Confessional Capital." In *The City in the Islamic World,* edited by Salma K. Jayyusi, Renata Holod, Attilio Petruccioli, and André Raymond, 221–45. Leiden: Brill, 2008.

Mikha'il, Murad. *al-A'mal al-Shi'riyya al-Kamila.* Shfram: Dar al-Mashriq, 1988.

al-Mozany, Hussain. "The Last Trip to Baghdad." *Banipal* 37 (2010): 6–19.

Muir, W. *The Caliphate, Its Rise, Decline, and Fall.* Edinburgh: John Grant, 1924.

Mustaghanimi, Ahlam. *al-Aswad Yaliqu Biki.* Beirut: Nawfal, 2012.

Muzaffar, May. *Layliyyat.* Amman: Dar al-Shuruq, 1994.

Nicholson, Reynold A. *A Literary History of the Arabs.* Cambridge: Cambridge University Press, 1956.

al-Nuwayri, Ahmad ibn 'Abd al-Wahhab. *Nihayat al-Arab fi Funun al-Adab.* Cairo: Wizarat al-Thaqafa wa-l-Irshad al-Qawmi and al-Mu'assasa al-Misriyya al-'Amma li-l-Ta'lif wa-l-Nashr, 1963–1998.

Ouyang, Wen-chin. *Literary Criticism in Medieval Arabic-Islamic Culture: The Making of a Tradition.* Edinburgh: Edinburgh University Press, 1997.

Ovadia, Ibrahim. *Sayha min 'Iraq al-'Ahd al-Ba'id.* Jerusalem: Rabitat al-Jami'iyyin al-Yahud al-Nazihim min al-'Iraq; Shfaram: Dar al-Mashriq, 1990.

Pamuk, Orhan. *Istanbul — Memories and the City.* Translated by Maureen Freely. New York: Vintage Books, 2006.

———. *The Museum of Innocence.* Translated by Maureen Freely. New York and Toronto: Alfred A. Knopf, 2009.

Qabbani, Nizar. *al-A'mal al-Shi'riyya al-Kamila.* Beirut: Manshurat Nizar Qabbani, 1997.

———. *al-A'mal al-Siyasiyya al-Kamila.* Beirut: Manshurat Nizar Qabbani, 1997.

al-Qasim, Samih. *Baghdad wa-Qasa'id Ukhra.* Nazareth: Manshurat Ida'at, 2008.

Rabinowitz, Dan, and Johnny Mansour. "Historicizing Climate: *Hayfawis* and *Haifo'im* Remembering the Winter of 1950." In *Haifa Before & After 1948: Narratives of a Mixed City,* edited by Mahmoud Yazbak and Yfaat Weiss, 119–48. Dordrecht: Institute for Historical Justice and Reconciliation, 2011.

Raymond, André. "Islamic City, Arab City: Orientalist Myths and Recent Views." *British Journal of Middle Eastern Studies* 21 (1994): 3–18.

————. *Arab Cities in the Ottoman Period: Cairo, Syria and the Maghreb*. Aldershot: Ashgate / Variorum, 2002.

Rejwan, Nissim. *The Jews of Iraq: 3000 Years of History and Culture*. London: Weidenfeld and Nicolson, 1985.

Riyad, Dalya. *'Asharat Alaf Lamhat Basar*. Beirut: Dar al-Saqi, 2008.

Roberts, Paul William. *The Demonic Comedy: Some Detours in the Baghdad of Saddam Hussein*. New York: Farrar, Straus and Giroux, 1998.

Rosen, Friedrich. *Oriental Memories of a German Diplomatist*. London: Methuen, 1930.

al-Rusafi, Ma'ruf. *Diwan*. Beirut: Dar al-'Awda, 1986.

al-Sabah, Su'ad. *al-Qasida Untha wa-l-Untha Qasida*. Kuwait: Dar Su'ad al-Sabah, 1999.

Sa'di, Muslih al-Din al-Shirazi. *Ash'aruhu al-'Arabiyya*. Edited by Ja'far Mu'yyad Shirazi. Beirut: al-Mu'assasa al-'Arabiyya li-l-Dirasat wa-l-Nashr, 1980.

al-Samarra'i, Majid. *Shadhil Taqa — Dirasa wa-Mukhtarat*. Beirut: al-Mu'assasa al-'Arabiyya li-l-Dirasat wa-l-Nashr, 1976.

Sassoon, David Solomon. *A History of the Jews in Baghdad*. Letchworth: S. D. Sassoon, 1949.

al-Sayyab, Badr Shakir. *Diwan*. Beirut: Dar al-'Awda, 1971.

Sedillot, L. A. *Histoire Générale des Arabes*. Paris: Maisonneuve, 1877.

Serjeant, R. B., ed. *The Islamic City (Selected Papers from the Colloquium Held at the Middle East Centre, Faculty of Oriental Studies, Cambridge, United Kingdom, from 19 to 23 July 1976)*. Paris: Unesco, 1980.

Shalash, Muhammad Jamil. *Diwan*. Beirut: Dar al-'Awda, 1978.

al-Sharif al-Radi. *Diwan*. Beirut: Dar Sadir, 1961.

Sha'ul, Anwar. *Qissat Hayati fi Wadi al-Rafidayn*. Jerusalem: Rabitat al-Jami'iyyin al-Yahud al-Nazihim min al-'Iraq, 1980.

————. *Wa-Bazagha Fajr Jadid*. Jerusalem: Rabitat al-Jami'iyyin al-Yahud al-Nazihim min al-'Iraq, 1983.

Shawqi, Ahmad. *Diwan*. Beirut: Dar al-Jil, 1995.

al-Shaykh, Manal. *Rasa'il La Tasilu*. Tunis: Fada'at, 2010.

Sheehi, Stephen. *Foundations of Modern Arab Identity*. Gainesville: University Press of Florida, 2004.

Smith, W. C. *Islam in Modern History*. New York: Mentor, 1963.

Snir, Reuven. "'We Were Like Those Who Dream': Iraqi-Jewish Writers in Israel in the 1950's." *Prooftexts* 11 (1991): 153–73.

———. "A Study of 'Elegy for al-Hallaj' by Adunis." *Journal of Arabic Literature* 25, no. 2 (1994a): 245–56.

———. "The 'World Upsidedown' in Modern Arabic Literature: New Literary Renditions of an Antique Religious Topos." *Edebiyat* 5 (1994b): 51–75.

———. "'My Heart Beats with Love of the Arabs': Iraqi Jews Writing in Arabic in the Twentieth Century." *Journal of Modern Jewish Studies* 1, no. 2 (2002): 182–203.

———. "'Forget Baghdad!': The Clash of Literary Narratives among Iraqi-Jews in Israel." *Orientalia Suecana* 53 (2004): 143–63.

———. *'Arviyut, Yahadut, Tsiyonut: Ma'avak Zehuyot ba-Yetsira shel Yehude 'Iraq*. Jerusalem: Ben-Zvi Institute, 2005.

———. "My Childhood Blossomed on the Waters of the Tigris": The Arabic Literature of Iraqi Jews in the 20th Century." *Bulletin of the Royal Institute for Inter-Faith Studies* (Amman) 8, nos. 1 and 2 (2006a): 29–68.

———. "'Religion Is for God, the Fatherland Is for Everyone': Arab-Jewish Writers in Modern Iraq and the Clash of Narratives after Their Immigration to Israel." *Journal of the American Oriental Society* 126, no. 3 (2006b): 379–99.

———. *Religion, Mysticism and Modern Arabic Literature*. Wiesbaden: Harrassowitz Verlag, 2006c.

———. "'Other Barbarians Will Come': Intertextuality, Meta-Poetry, and Meta-Myth in Mahmud Darwish's Poetry." In *Mahmoud Darwish, Exile's Poet: Critical Essays*, edited by Hala Khamis Nassar and Najat Rahman, 123–66. Northampton, MA: Interlink Books, 2008.

Someck, Ronny. *Gan Eden le-Orez*. Tel Aviv: Zmora-Bitan, 1996.

———. *Koah Sus*. Tel Aviv: Zmora-Bitan, 2013.

Somekh, Sasson. *Baghdad, Yesterday: The Making of an Arab Jew*. Jerusalem: Ibis Editions, 2007.

Stark, Freya. *Baghdad Sketches: Journeys through Iraq*. London: Tauris Parke Paperbacks, 2011.

Stetkevych, Jaroslav. *The Zephyrs of Najd: The Poetics of Nostalgia in the Classical Arabic Nasib*. Chicago: University of Chicago Press, 1993.

al-Subaki, Taj al-Din. *Tabaqat al-Shafi'iyya al-Kubra*. Edited by Mahmud Mahmud al-Tanaji and 'Abd al-Fattah Muhammad al-Hilu. Cairo: 'Isa al-Babai al-Halabi, 1964–68.

Sumi, Akiko Motoyoshi. *Description in Classical Arabic Poetry: Wasf, Ekphrasis, and Interarts Theory*. Leiden: Brill, 2004.

al-Suyuti, Jalal al-Din. *al-Muzhir fi 'Ulum al-Lugha wa-Anwa'iha*. Cairo: Dar Ihya' al-Kutub al-'Arabiyya, n.d.

———. *Ta'rikh al-Khulafa'*. Cairo: Dar Nahdat Misr, 1976.

Tejel, Jordi, Peter Sluglett, Riccardo Bocco, Hamit Bozarslan, eds. *Writing the Modern History of Iraq: Historiographical and Political Challenges*. Singapore: World Scientific Publishing, 2012.

al-Tha'alibi, 'Abd al-Malik ibn Muhammad. *Yatimat al-Dahr fi Shu'ara' Ahl al-'Asr*. Damascus: al-Matba'a al-Hafniyya, 1885.

———. *Yatimat al-Dahr fi Mahasin Ahl al-'Asr*. Cairo: al-Maktaba al-Tijariyya al-Kubra, 1956.

Tibawi, A. L. *Islamic Education: Its Traditions and Modernization into the Arab National Systems*. London: Luzac, 1972.

Toorawa, Shawkat M. *Ibn Abi Tahir Tayfur and Arabic Writerly Culture: A Ninth-Century Bookman in Baghdad*. London: RoutledgeCurzon, 2005.

Touhmazi, 'Abd al-Rahman. *Akthar min Nash'atin li-Wahidin fa-Hasb*. Cologne: Al-Kamel Verlag, 1995.

Von Grunebaum. G. E. *Modern Islam: The Search for Cultural Identity*. Berkeley and Los Angeles: University of California Press, 1962.

———. *Islam: Essays in the Nature and Growth of a Cultural Tradition*. London: Routledge & Kegan Paul, 1969.

Vuong, Hoa Hoï, and Patrick Mégarbané. *Le dîwân de Bagdad: le siècle d'or de la poésie arabe.* Arles: Actes Sud, 2007.

al-Wardi, 'Ali. *Lamahat Ijtima'iyya min Ta'rikh al-'Iraq al-Hadith.* Baghdad: Matba'at al-Irshad, 1971.

Warren, John, and Ihsan Fethi. *Traditional Houses in Baghdad.* Horsham, UK: Coach Publishing House, 1982.

al-Washsha', Abu al-Tayyib Muhammad ibn Ishaq ibn Yahya. *al-Muwashsha' aw al-Zarf wa-l-Zurafa'.* Beirut: Dar Sadir and Dar Beirut, 1965.

Wasserstrom, Steven M. *Between Muslim and Jew: The Problem of Symbiosis under Early Islam.* Princeton: Princeton University Press, 1995.

Wellsted, J. R. *Travels in the City of the Caliphs.* London: Henry Colburn, 1840.

Wiet, Gaston. *Introduction à la littérature arabe.* Paris: Maisonneuve et Larose, 1966.

Yaqut al-Hamawi al-Baghdadi. *Mu'jam al-Buldan.* Edited by Farid 'Abd al-'Aziz al-Jundi. Beirut: Dar al-Kutub al-'Ilmiyya, 1990.

Yusuf, Sa'di. *Diwan.* Beirut: Dar al-'Awda, 1988.

———. *al-A'mal al-Shi'riyya.* Nicosia: Dar al-Mada li-l-Thaqafa wa-l-Nashr, 1995.

———. *al-A'mal al-Shi'riyya.* Cologne: Al-Kamel Verlag, 2009.

al-Zahawi, Jamil Sidqi. *Diwan.* Beirut: Dar al-'Awda, 1972.

Zurayk, Constantine K. *The Meaning of the Disaster.* Beirut: Khayat, 1956.

Index of Poets

Index of Titles